Alan G. Thompson

The
Naked Counsellor

authorHOUSE™

1663 LIBERTY DRIVE, SUITE 200
BLOOMINGTON, INDIANA 47403
(800) 839-8640
WWW.AUTHORHOUSE.COM

First published by AuthorHouse 11/28/05

ISBN: 1-4208-8109-4 (sc)

Printed in the United States of America
Bloomington, Indiana

This book is printed on acid-free paper.

Table of Contents

PREFACE   vii

CHAPTER 1   INTRODUCTION   1

CHAPTER 2   ATTENTION, VIEW POINTS
            AND IDENTITIES   6

CHAPTER 3   WHAT DO YOU WANT?
            WHO WOULD YOU LIKE TO BE?   14

CHAPTER 4   BRINGING SUCCESS INTO YOUR LIFE   26

CHAPTER 5   HOW TO TALK TO YOURSELF
            AND TO OTHERS THROUGH THE
            FIVE ELEMENTS OF A PERSON   41

CHAPTER 6   THE SECRETS OF SUCCESSFUL PERSON-
            TO-PERSON COMMUNICATION   54

CHAPTER 7   MAKING FRIENDS - RELATIONSHIPS
            AND CONTROL   77

CHAPTER 8   YOUR AND OTHER PEOPLE'S IDENTITIES   89

CHAPTER 9   MOTIVATING PEOPLE TO DO
            WHAT YOU WANT THEM TO DO   98

CHAPTER 10 TWO MIRACULOUS SOURCES OF POWER   114

PREFACE

This book is essentially an intellectual approach to a number of topics that might be termed life sustaining. It is concerned with telling oneself things rather than feeling them. For most readers, some of the material will be familiar. To try to delineate a comprehensive picture, not everything will be a revelation – in fact, most of it is common sense. It is inevitable that I have picked up a lot of ideas in my long life from other people's thoughts and writings and I gratefully acknowledge my debt   There is no copyright in ideas but where I have quoted, I have endeavoured to make it clear that they are quotations and have given the appropriate acknowledgements. I believe there are some original contributions..

I am quite old although I do not feel it and have accumulated a good deal of experience of life. I have been married twice. The first time, for almost twenty five years, when my first wife, Madge, the mother of four of my children, died. I have been very fortunate in having a second wife, Joy, the mother of my fifth child. Both wives have given me great advice and support and both have accomplished the trick of keeping my feet on the ground and, at the same time, keeping me on my toes.

Most of the ideas concerning communication and relationships that I write about in this book have come about not only from counselling individuals but from my work as a management consultant, resolving conflict in large organisations. Much I write about takes place between one person and another, but this can also be applied to two groups of people whether they are few in number or nations, where negotiations have to occur and agreement has to be strived for and hopefully achieved.

It is hoped that this book will be helpful and useful. I am aware that it probably has many shortcomings and omissions but lack the objectivity to discover and correct them. I am sanguine that my readership will do so. I will be grateful for criticisms, suggestions, and advice, the results of which I will incorporate in a future edition, if the initial reception of the book merits it.

CHAPTER 1

INTRODUCTION

Why naked?

We are all naked under our clothes but most of the time we are not aware of this, and even if we are, we don't feel as exposed as we would do, if we were really naked. Often our clothes are designed, not only to keep us warm and unexposed, but also to be the props to support our self-image and the image we wish to project. However, being without clothes, especially out of doors, gives most people a sense of freedom, of being more at one with nature. It can be a coming into communication with our body, making friends with it, becoming more aware of it and what we are doing to it.

Just as we conceal our bodies, from ourselves as well as others, so we also hide our psychological selves with a collection of identities, roles, attitudes, fears, and prejudices. They serve a similar purpose for our psyche as do our clothes for our body. They hide our psychological nakedness and support the way we present ourselves to the outside world. Ultimately in life, we are alone and naked and whatever thoughts and communications come to us, we have to counsel ourselves. So we are all naked counsellors.

Counselling

Counselling someone largely consists of asking questions and listening to the answers. It is undertaken to allow the person being counselled to unburden her/himself and to be able to look dispassionately and objectively at the answers she/he is giving and thus gain a better understanding of whatever is involved.

It is possible to counsel yourself. This is what this book is going to enable you to do. However, it may be that you will not always ask the right questions and may shy away from the challenging question that you really ought to ask yourself.

For this book to do what it can do – that is, enable you to achieve whatever you reasonably want - it is essential that you face up to the questions and, more importantly, face up to the answers. Psychological change is generally accompanied by emotion. No upset and generally this means nothing significant has happened. There has been no sudden insight, no 'wow' factor, no 'Gosh, now I see it'. So, do not be concerned but be pleased if you have feelings or emotions whilst working through the self counselling exercises that are to be found throughout the book.

The Naked Counsellor

This book is designed to enable you, the reader, to counsel yourself about a number of topics that are fundamental to your success in life. There are a series of Chapters, each of which deals with a life enhancing topic. At the end of each Chapter there are a series of questions entitled 'Self Counselling'. You ask yourself the questions and look at the answers.

If the activity of questioning and looking at the answers is to be effective and successful, you need to try to be psychologically naked – that is, open to whatever comes into your mind and as far as possible unburdened by worries, prejudices and fears and able to step outside the roles you play and identities you assume. It is important that you become more yourself, the real you.

When you divest yourself of your clothes – at night or to shower or bathe – it may be helpful to see this as a series of symbolic acts of getting rid of your psychological clothes. As you take off each garment, you can imagine freeing yourself from the pressures of the day, the discarding of who you have to be, what you have to do. However, this is not essential. You can get rid of your psychological clothes anywhere and at any time.

More about what the book is about

This divesting of the psychological garments is not as easy to accomplish as taking off our physical clobber. You have probably become entangled with much of it. One purpose of this book is to enable you to engage in a process of untangling, so that you become more of a Naked Counsellor.

It is also designed to help you to improve your ability to do what you want to do, to help you to improve communicating and making friends with yourself and with others. It is about achieving material success but also about creating and experiencing love and happiness, making your nearest and dearest happier, healthier and more successful, as well as yourself.

It deals with what you need to know about topics that will help you to be more successful, communicate more effectively, relate to and motivate other people. It recognises that reading all the success books in the world will not alone make you successful. It is necessary to take the ideas into your being and counsel yourself to make sure that you have made the necessary attitude and mind-set changes. This is when, as the Naked Counsellor, freeing yourself from the entanglement of your psychological clothes, you ask yourself the right questions, look and listen to the answers and decide what you need to do as a result.

Achieving what you want to achieve, will necessitate you communicating with and relating to other people. Throughout the book this is simplified to you communicating with and interacting with one other person. That other person is me - but clearly, it can be anyone. The ideas and principles can be extended beyond this person-to-person communication and interaction to groups of any size.

As you read the Chapters, thoughts and ideas will come into your mind. Do try to capture these by writing them down in the blank pages at the end of the book, because they are your very own. If you complete answering the Self Counselling questions by recording them in the spaces provided, you will personalise the book, adding value and making it of special worth.

Outline of the Book

Chapter 2 Attention, View points and identities

Moving your attention around to different view points – from the present to the past or the future, as well as from here to anywhere. You can visit other people's view points. You can assume identities. You can occupy other people's identities without getting stuck in them. The pluses and minuses of identities

Chapter 3 What you want? Who do you want to be?

What you would like to happen in your life, if there were nothing to stop you. Who can help you to get where you want to be?
Making a detailed action plan to achieve what you want

Chapter 4 Bringing success into your life
How Positive and how Negative you are, and how to emphasise the Positive and kill off the Negative.
Assumptions about Positive and Negative. The reservoir. Positive thinking ideas.
Making positive declarations that will achieve success for you.
Visualising success.

Chapter 5 How to talk to yourself and to others through the five elements of a person
Understanding the 5 elements of a person - the body, the mind, the Positive, the Negative and the spirit. How they communicate with each other and with the five elements of someone else. Communicating with yourself - your body, mind, Positive and Negative.

Chapter 6 The secrets of successful person-to-person communication
21 ways of getting across to someone what you want them to do and 8 things not to do.
Being aware of the hidden messages - the meta messages.
10 things to do to listen effectively
Understanding the power of giving and receiving attention and being in the 'here-and-now'.
Negotiating successfully.

Chapter 7 Making friends – relationships and control
Making friends and establishing relationships. Relationships and control.
Measuring the strength of a relationship.
Some good ways of solving relationship problems.

Chapter 8 Your and other people's identities
3 important identities – Controller, Influencer, and Compliant. Understanding how they communicate with each other enables you to solve many human relation problems,
Jung's psychological types.

Chapter 9 Motivating people to do what you want them to do

4 sorts of motivation – material rewards, material deprivations, psychological rewards and psychological deprivations.

Releasing energy by achieving agreement - within yourself, within groups and within organisations.

Resolving disagreements – negotiations.

6 ways of getting someone to agree with you.

Chapter 10 Two fantastic sources of power

Understanding what love is and how to give and receive it.

Tapping into the power of the Universal Intelligence.

CHAPTER 2

ATTENTION, VIEW POINTS AND IDENTITIES

Paying or giving attention is essential in most human activities, whether it is listening to someone or something, operating a machine, playing a game or watching the television. It is a sort of looking, although more than sight may be involved or it may not involve sight at all - for example, when you are listening to the radio. The words 'paying' and 'giving' are interesting for the implication that the activity is costing you something. If you are giving all your attention, then you are giving a great deal by losing your identity, temporarily, to the thing to which you are giving attention. It is an essential part of listening and therefore, of communicating. It is one of your primary activities. If you are not paying attention to something you are day-dreaming or asleep.

You can move your attention around. It is like the pointer on a computer screen. You can give your attention to, say, the television and to what is happening on the screen. Someone comes into the room. You withdraw your attention from the television and give it to your visitor. Do you turn the television off or do you leave it on? Perhaps you just turn the sound off but leave the picture flickering away. Perhaps you have not really withdrawn all of your attention from what is happening on the television. It may be the last few minutes of a tennis match. You have a choice to withdraw your attention from the screen and move it to the visitor, but to be able to do this requires there to be a separation between you and what you are giving attention to. Otherwise, you become entangled with the object of your attention so that you can no longer separate your attention. Maybe this is what is happening with the tennis match. You cannot tear yourself away from it. You are temporarily an obsessive viewer. So you either pretend to give attention to your visitor or explain to her/ him that you would dearly like to see the end of the tennis match. However, if you can avoid such entanglement, you can turn the television off and give all your attention to your visitor.

You can move your attention from the present to the past or the future, as well as from here to anywhere. It can view ideas, thoughts within yourself or outside. Once again the phenomena of entanglement can occur. Your mind may keep on going back to something that happened in the past. You can't get it out of your mind.. Or it may be that you are continually crossing some bridge in the future - a job interview, an operation, a driving test. Your attention is trapped. If this is so, it is one of the psychological garments you have to discard to become the independent, Naked Counsellor.

View points.

Where your attention is, is where you are. For example, imagine you are thinking about and giving attention to an incident in the past - the day you passed an examination, for example. If you are giving this your full attention, you are there in front of the results notice board and there is your name and against one subject, which you thought you would fail, there is the word 'pass'. You can see your contemporaries crowding around you, some expressing dismay, others whooping with delight. At this moment you are back there at University and this is, temporarily, the place where you are. 'Place', in the sense I would like to use the word, may not necessarily be a physical location but an argument, an idea, a work of art, anywhere your attention can be. Just as your attention moves, so you move to a new place.

If this happens, you may delude yourself into thinking that it is an old, familiar, comfortable place where you have been many times before. You will then see what you used to see from the old place and be unable to see the realities facing you from the new place. This is a not infrequent human experience. For example, you may join a new social group that has different rules of behavior from those with which you are familiar. You may retain your old ideas about rules of behavior that have served you well in the past, even though someone is trying to shift you to a new place. Before long, experience will teach you that what someone has been trying to tell you is a fact - you are in a new situation.

People get stuck in a particular place. You have only to look at the conflicts in the world to see many examples of two groups of people stuck in places, hurling words and, more often than not, missiles at each other. They behave as if they were in trenches and unable to get out. Their separate places or view points are frequently a matter of faith rather than of fact and this makes it particularly difficult to achieve agreement. If only one lot could climb out of their trench and go and occupy the other people's trench, they might understand why the other people think as they do. If the other people paid a return visit, some mutual understanding might follow. Similar principles are inferred in the idea of stepping into the other person's shoes. As Robbie

Burns said 'O wad some Pow'r, the giftie gie us, to see oursels as others see us! It wad frae mony a blunder free us...'

To avoid the entanglement of your attention, you have to be able to move it and to be detached. The skill in all this, is a matter of will power and of self-control. This is easier said than done. Only too readily we become obsessed with something or someone. It may be with the need to have another cigarette or bar of chocolate or orgasm. Our attention is seized and we feel unable to separate our self from the object of our desire. We cease to be free but become a slave. We become the place our attention is entangled with. A piece of old fashioned advice often proffered to young people setting out in the world, about how to behave was 'keep your distance'. In other words, 'keep separate so that you can disengage when you wish'. When the distance between you and what you are looking at, shrinks to nothing, you then become what you are giving your attention to. You become the place. I call this 'identification'. To be the Naked Counsellor you need to avoid being stuck in any place or view point.

Identification

Ask someone who they are and you may get a sequence of answers along the following lines.

> 'I'm Joe Bloggs of 34 XYZ Terrace, Downtown, Anyoldwhere.'
> 'Who else are you?
> 'I'm Martha's husband and the father of Samantha and Joseph.'
> 'Who else are you?'
> 'I'm Sales Director of Bloggs Technical Services Ltd.'.
> 'And who else?'
> 'I am a member of Anyoldwhere Golf Club'.
> 'And who else?'
> 'I am the owner of a Jaguar car'.

and so it might run on, and on. These are all identities, places where Joe is from time to time and it is possible that Joe thinks that the sum total of these add up to being him. But if Joe loses his house and his wife and children and his business, his membership of the club and the car, there is still Joe, the person who has assumed the identities. If Joe is locked into these identities, he may find it difficult to identify with someone who is unmarried and has no children, who is a manual worker, belonging to the local fishing club and owning an old motor-bike. But if Joe can be detached from his identities and can answer, when asked who he is, 'I am me', he has the possibility of being able to put himself in the position of anyone he chooses and hence understand how things seem to anyone else - in other words, to be able to occupy anyone else's place or space. This is the situation the Naked Counsellor has to achieve.

There is a human need to assume identities. It may stem from people's lack of certainty of who they are. It is not very interesting to be a nonentity and it can be unpleasant to have doubts about one's existence. So identities are assumed like clothes. These also enable other people to know who you are. A person can also feel a need for an adequate mix of identities which makes him unique, different from anyone else. If everyone had the same identities, one person would be indistinguishable from another and this would be almost as bad as not having an identity at all. It is important to realise that your identities are predominantly ones that you have given yourself.

This compulsive attachment to a number of fixed places and identities can be a great source of strength in some situations - for example, in time of war. 'I am British, a soldier, a patriot, a hater of the enemy and so on'. It can also lead to great bigotry and fanaticism, possibly culminating, for example, in racial hatred and ethnic cleansing.

This assumption of identities is a form of differentiation which may make agreement with those not having similar identities, very difficult. People with similar identities collect together, so identities can be positive in bringing people together. However, much conflict on both the personal, group and national level is concerned with differentiation. These may be racial where the identification is with appearance, location, language and customs. Even more intransigent conflicts arise when the identifications are with beliefs such as occur with religions.

At the personal level, once you and the thing you are giving your attention to, are absolutely and entirely one, you have assumed an identity and your ability to control what you are identifying with is greatly diminished. The 'thing' may be external - another person, group, physical object. - or it may be internal - an idea, obsession, fear and so on.

You, like anyone else, can be what you believe yourself to be - in the sense that you can completely identify with a particular vision. Then as far as you are concerned, you are that vision. You are stuck in this place but it may not be one shared with anyone else. For example, if you believe that you are

Marie Antoinette, it is unlikely that anyone else will share your view. But if you passionately believe that you are a crusader to achieve the banning of all cruel sports, you will not be alone. You may identify so completely with your vision of yourself that you will stop at nothing to realise your objective. Others may not be so dedicated even though they can share your place, where you are coming from, for unlike you, they are not entangled in it.

Much good and much evil has been generated in the world by people stuck in particular points of view. To achieve, it is often believed to be necessary to have an internal conviction and to avoid the weakening of resolve which comes from seeing alternatives. This is a perfectly valid approach. The danger with conviction politics at any level is that it can lead to a lack of realism and the adherence to ideas that are shared by a diminishing number of people. Nevertheless, there are situations where compromise is not possible, where there is no common ground and where it is impossible to occupy a place with which one is not in conflict with someone else.

So the important thing is to realise that a place is just that - it is somewhere that you are at the moment and from which you can move away. You can visit other people's points of view and so get a more multi-dimensional picture. You can assume identities and occupy other people's identities without getting stuck in them. This requires you to be conscious of any identity you assume and means avoiding inappropriate emotion - you have to be in a detached and positive frame of mind, to abandon your identities and view points and become the Naked Counsellor.

Self Counselling No. 2.1 Points of view and identity

Before undertaking an important communication, consider and think about the following, for yourself and whoever you are going to communicate with.

Your points of view

Can you move out of them?

What do you think her/his points of view are?

Do you think she/he can move out of them?

What identities do you have?

Which ones are you entangled with i.e. cannot separate from?

What identities does she/he have?

Which ones do you think she/he is entangled with?

What does the above mean for each of those you wish to communicate with?

CHAPTER 3

WHAT DO YOU WANT? WHO WOULD YOU LIKE TO BE?

So what would you like to happen?

The purpose of this Book is to help you to realise your ambitions, to make happen what you want to happen. So the first thing to do is to be clear about what you really want? This is a challenging question. Many of us voice ambitions or wishes but follow them up with all the reasons why they cannot happen or fear about what the consequences might be. If you could become rich without having to deal with people, you would probably grab it with both hands. So many people gamble on the lottery or in other ways, to prosper without having to interact with people.

If you want a more certain route, it is inevitable that you will have to become involved with people and almost certainly with responsibilities, decisions and risk. It is essential to think through what you want to happen, what might happen, and how to avoid getting the wrong outcome.

For example you might want to become a fashion model. You have the right figure and face and you know that a successful model can become very wealthy. Firstly you have to find an agency which will take you on. Before that you have to have good photographs taken which will cost you. You have heard that some agencies exploit, using young women as 'hostesses'. What price are you willing to pay? Are you ready to leave home? There are nearly always risks and unknowns.

Putting all such fears and possible limitations aside, what would you really like to happen? What do you want out of life? Perhaps you would like to get rid of the mortgage, have a better job, a new car, become a multimillionaire. Maybe you want to get married, have a book published. Perhaps you want to have a better relationship with your child or parent or friend. Or you want to become a successful politician or travel. Your objectives may be in terms of the job you would like - game warden in Africa, an internationally recognised chef, detective, journalist, airline pilot. What you want need not be earth shattering but, at the same time, do not be too modest. This part of the exercise can be great fun and also quite self revealing.

As soon as you start to do this, you start to think of obstacles, limitations, reasons why what you would like to happen would never be possible, so it might be useful to look at these.

Limitations

Limitations may be real or imaginary. A real one may be illness. If you have a debilitating disease then the limitations may be severe. Nevertheless, even in the direst circumstances, it is possible to think of something you would like to have or to do. You might have lesser disabilities like asthma, diabetes or a bad back, which may make it impossible to compete in some physical activities We are often inspired by the courage of those severely disabled who, for example, write books with the aid of computers or take part in wheelchair marathons. Possibly you are in captivity but prisoners take degrees, write books, learn new skills. So even real limitations, and there are many different sorts, need not be as limiting as they might seem to be at first sight.

Many limitations are imaginary. Fear is perhaps the most debilitating of these. It comes in many guises - fear of falling assails most of us. Physically it can be real enough.. 'I could never climb a 50 foot vertical ladder. I would get vertigo or have a heart attack.' Many people fear to take actions to better themselves because of a fear of failure, of losing face. Falling from 50 feet would probably kill you. Failing to secure agreement to some plan you are proposing is not life threatening but you may behave as though it is. For some, losing a job is like losing a life but in reality it is often the opposite, the beginning of a new and exciting activity. Fear sometimes protects you from doing something disastrous but a lot of the time it stops you doing what would be best for you.

Having children to look after or caring for an old relative may limit what you can do. Maybe you have principles that you regard as sacrosanct. The first time you start to write down what you would like to happen, try to cast all limitations aside, even if this seems unrealistic. Then look at the limitations, the boundaries. How many of these limitations could be eliminated, how many boundaries widened? What would it take?

Materialism

We live in a very materialistic world where success is often measured in terms of money and possessions. Following the ideas in this Book may well result in material success but remember there may be a price to pay. Possessions exert their own tyranny. A car has to be maintained, a yacht to be sailed, houses to be visited, money to be invested and monitored, cigarettes to be smoked. You have to weigh up the price, to see if the happiness and contentment you expect makes it worthwhile.

Rich and famous people often do not appear to be much happier or content than those one meets in the slums of Delhi or Colombo. It is just possible that a search for wealth, power and glory may actually be a search for happiness and contentment. Many people think one leads to the other but it is clear that it does not always do so.

A man who had built an international business from scratch, told me that he had enjoyed the challenge and the intricacies of the business game but that at the end of his career he had great regrets that he had neglected his family and had failed to enjoy the love and happiness that he knew could have been his. Success may be a mix of goals achieved, some of which may not be material but more concerned with care, nurturing, love and relationships.

Self Counselling -Your goals

Self Counselling questions follow below to help you decide what you want to happen. This is a process that you can keep on revising as time goes on but if you make a start now, it should help to motivate you to pursue the learning process that this Book sets in motion.

It is worth repeating the advice to put on one side the difficulties or limitations that will come to mind as you set your targets. Doing so can make you feel that you are being unrealistic as they may seem so far beyond what is possible. However, although not all of them may come true, it is surprising how often the more important ones do.

You will probably want to revise the answers you write on the Self Counselling questionnaires in this Book. If so, photocopy them as many times as you like or copy them onto your computer.

The first group of questions address your immediate needs

What would I like to happen now?
What possessions would I like to acquire now?
What job or profession would I like to be following now?
What skills would I like to acquire now?

The second group of questions asks you to take a look at any period you like to specify in the future, say three years ahead.

The Self Counselling sections are numbered in relation to the Chapters of the book to which they refer. There are no Self Counselling sections numbered '1'.

Self Counselling No.3.1

What would I like to happen now?

What possessions would I like to acquire now?

What job or profession would I like to be following now?

What skills would I like to possess now?

Self Counseling No 3.2

What would I like to happen over the next........years?

What possessions would I like to acquire over the next ...... years?

What job or profession would I like to be following in …………..years time?

What skills would I like to possess in ……..years time?

Action plans

For each of the goals you have, you need to develop a list of actions and the names of individuals, and perhaps groups, who will assist you. Number each goal and put it at the head of a blank piece of A4. Then list the actions, numbering each one of them

As an example, let's say that one of your objectives is to write a book and get it published

At the head of the blank A4 write

Goal A - To write a book on Crocodiles and get it published

Actions

A.1.   Write the first two or three chapters of the book and a reasonably detailed synopsis of the remainder of the book.

A.2.   Find an agent who will look at it and persuade her/him that it is worth consideration.

A.3.   Take aboard your agent's and everyone else's criticism.

A.4.   Rewrite all or some of the book.

A.5.   Repeat (1.3) and (1.4) until you can.

A.6.   Persuade your agent to look for a publisher.

A.7.   Persuade the publisher, that there will be many people who want to read the book.

A.8.   If and when the publisher decides to publish, respond to the copy editor's criticisms, i.e. possibly rewrite some of the material.

A.9.   When the book is about to be published, answer all the marketing people's questions.

A.10. Get the book reviewed by as many publications as possible.

The things other people need to do for action A.1:

A.1.1   Your nearest and dearest, to put up with you spending many hours in your room, when there are so many other things needing to be done.

A.1.2   Your friend Bill, son Jack, daughter Jane to read what you have written and to make constructive criticisms.

The things you need to get other people to do for action A.1.1

You have to convince your nearest and dearest that the book will be a great success and that all your effort and time will pay off. You have, incidentally, to convince yourself of this. You also may have to be more enthusiastic and supportive of her/his activities, as a quid pro quo.

For A.1.2 to work, you have to convince Bill, Jack and Jane that you will take aboard their criticisms and ideas, before they will take the effort to read what you have written.

The things you need to get other people to do for action A 2:

A.2.1   You may be fortunate in having an agent but if you haven't you will have to write, Email, fax or telephone each of those agents likely to be interested in your book and persuade her/him to read and get an expert opinion on it. You can find the addresses of agents by consulting the writer's handbooks in the local library.

A.2.2   You have to respond to the criticisms

and so on as you go on down the list. If you have a computer, it is easy to update and modify this list as you proceed with your project.

You may find the Action Schedule below useful to organise and monitor your action plan.

ACTION SCHEDULE

Reference....................

Date..........................

Sent to Date					

Activity.......................................

No.	Action	Responsible	Date	Comments

To summarise, having identified those with whom you have to communicate, and what you have to persuade them to do, you need to review, one by one, how you are going to do it. You might think what their objections might be and how you are going to overcome them. You may find this somewhat bureaucratic assembly of forms helpful particularly in the early stages of realising your goal but it is possible you can simplify the process as you go along. This starts off a process of learning and obtaining information, which produces more ideas about who to contact and the development of whatever it is you are wishing to promote.

You need to keep these Forms 3.1 and 3.2 up to date because you will be referring back to them as you work through subsequent Chapters.

The next Chapter is about your attitude - how positive is it and the actions you can take to improve your chances of achieving the goals you have set yourself in this Chapter.

CHAPTER 4

BRINGING SUCCESS INTO YOUR LIFE

'EMPHASISE THE POSITIVE. KILL OFF THE NEGATIVE.

Positive and Negative

A good starting point to think about achieving success, is to consider the ideas implied by the concepts *positive* and **negative**. Down the ages, these have been personified in mythology, folklore and religions as, for example, good fairies and witches, angels and demons. The greatest negative of them all has been manifest as the Devil and the greatest positive as God or one of other religion's equivalents.

Some of the good things that are meant by 'Positive' are being happy, loving, creative, optimistic, friendly, forgiving, agreeable. They infer enthusiasm, cheerfulness, hope and attributes such as honesty, trust and faith.

What is meant by 'Negative' is the opposite of Positive and is, for example, bad, unhappy, hating, apathetic, destructive, despairing, pessimistic, unfriendly, miserable, distrustful, untrustworthy, disagreeable, brutal, sadistic.

Positive is like the sun, the light. Negative is dark, like the night. Both exist outside each one of us, Positively, in the form of love, support and gains: and Negatively as fear, threats and losses. Both also exist inside us - our hopes and doubts reflecting our vision of the outside world, supplemented by our imagination.

Positive seems to generate an upward spiral. Positive attitudes work to disarm Negative emotions, such as fear and anger, which often cause incorrect decisions to be made. Positive attitudes promote hopeful, confident, enthusiastic feelings. These, in turn, increase the likelihood of achieving goals, gains, and success. If these occur, they reinforce Positive attitudes and actions and so the upward spiral continues. Success breeds success. Observing successful people often confirms this theory, although it is possible sometimes to see the seeds of failure being sown if prosperity gives rise to overconfidence or over indulgence.

The downward spiral is a mirror image of the Positive one. Negative seems to generate unhelpful emotions which can result in irrational decisions or no decisions at all. These can lead to failure and losses, which increase the amount of Negative in the situation and the downward spiral continues. However, just as success can lead to overconfidence, so failure can sometimes generate a will to succeed and a reversal of the spiral.

During a day we experience both Positive and Negative. The morning post may bring bills and bad news. Shrugging these off, things may go well at work, an important client comes into the shop and at long last, buys. Going to lunch you bump into an old friend, whose address you had lost. You have a super lunch and a lot of laughs. Back at work you are ticked off for getting back late. You find you have forgotten to re-order some items which have now run out of stock. Back home and your daughter is in a foul mood having had a bad day at school. Your partner comes in with a bottle of wine and some steak and volunteers to get supper. You go out to put the car away and find it will not start.

This is typical. The sun comes out and goes in and is replaced by clouds and rain. Over a longer period, you may experience a run of Negative events - they rarely seem to come singly. Someone you love dies, you lose your job, the car needs replacing, you fall and break your leg. One damn thing after another and there seems no end to it. It is easy and not unreasonable to be cast down by this turn of events, to believe that you are dogged by bad luck, that whatever you do will turn out badly.

But a year later, it may all be different. You have a good win on some speculation, you have a better job, your daughter wins a scholarship and your partner gets a promotion. Now the sun is shining and you feel good. You start to get creative ideas and believe that you are now blessed with good luck.

Certainly, favourable and unfavourable happenings seem to bunch, as is evident in popular sayings such as 'It never rains but what it pours', 'Troubles never come singly', or by Shakespeare: 'There is a tide in the affairs of men, which, taken at the flood, leads on to fortune'. This bunching was studied by the psychiatrist C.G.Jung, who produced supporting evidence for the idea.

He gave it the name 'Synchronicity'. and it seems to be a real phenomena which most of us have experienced.

Many of the fortunes made by individuals have been the result of a long a run of good luck. Many years ago, Caroline Otero, at the roulette table in Monte Carlo, put her last two 20-franc pieces on 'red' and walked away from the table, thinking they would go the same way as all her previous bets. However, red came up 28 times in a row, the bank was broken and she had made a fortune. She must subsequently have had a run of bad luck because she died penniless. Winning streaks do exist, as do losing streaks. You tend only to hear of the big successes and wonder why you cannot follow in their footsteps. But many people become bankrupt and companies go into liquidation. Examples of the 'bunching' effect are often seen when tragic accidents occur, for example, at sea or in aircraft, when often a number of things go wrong at the same time.

In this book we are often concerned with motivating, persuading and forming a relationship with another person. To make this come alive, the central person in the book is you and the other person is me.

Assumptions of positive and negative

When you and I are at the beginning of a relationship, both you and I can make assumptions about ourselves and about the other, as to being Positive or Negative. For example, you may assume the identity of someone having all the Positive attributes - 'I'm alright, I'm a good guy' and you may make the same assumptions about me - 'You're alright, You're a good guy'. This is a very hopeful and desirable attitude and if these assumptions are mirrored by me, we should get along well.

However, you might assume you are alright but attribute a Negative identity to me. You may be a policeman and assume that I am an undesirable, up to no good. You may be a teacher and I, a pupil and assume that I am lazy and unmotivated. This probably does not provide a good starting point for a relationship or constructive communication.

Less likely but possible, you may assume a Negative identity but attribute to me a Positive one. This is the sort of self-effacing attitude you might adopt if you felt that you were of no value and that I was important. Again, not auguring well for a good relationship.

Finally, for completeness, you might think both of us are not alright. 'We're both a couple of losers. Nothing will ever come right for us'. This might form some sort of basis for communication but it is not likely to be very constructive.

These are stated from your point of view. There is another identical set of possibilities from my point of view. So, for example, both you and I might be thinking 'I'm Positive, you're not Positive', based on appearance, hearsay, where you come from. This is a recipe for disagreement. It is obviously best for both people in an important conversation to start off with the mutual assumptions: 'We are both Positive people'. You, personally, can at least start off with this assumption and if I don't agree, you will need to work on it. Bear in mind that there is also the possibility that the assumptions we are making about each other may be wide of the mark. You may think my assumption about you is that I think 'I'm Positive, you're Negative' whereas it might be 'We are both Negative'.

This attribution of the identities of being Positive or Negative to other people is often a sort of knee-jerk reaction, a gut feeling, a first impression, which can in fact be wide of the mark. Criticism often has the implication 'I'm better than you'.

As soon as possible in an exchange of views, it is important to convey to the other person, for example me, that you think I am alright and to discover what I am assuming about you. If you think I am making Negative assumptions about you, which you think are untrue, it is necessary to clear up these false impressions, as soon as you possibly can.

It is important to identify correctly, individuals or groups that are basically Negative, destructive, dishonest, evil. Negativity is catching. There are many examples that this is so from history or from the media most days.

As to the relationships you already have, you have the choice with each person to identify, celebrate and feel grateful for the Positive elements in her/his character and behavior or to concentrate on her/his Negative aspects and feel aggrieved and downcast as a result. What you do is your choice and what you tell yourself as a result of making the choice is not necessarily true but is what you are telling yourself.

The resevoir

Quite apart from, but affected, by Positive and Negative external events, is the internal flow of Positive and Negative, in the mind. It is as though there is a reservoir which may at a particular time be full of the Positive, full of light, if you like. Either, because of what happens outside of you or what you may be thinking, the Negative begins to flow into the reservoir. This Negative displaces the Positive either partly or wholly. You can see this happening to other people or to a group or even to a nation. So this possibility of change during the development of a relationship between two people, in the short or long run, is another complication in the interplay of assumptions and identities of Positive and Negative discussed above.

Watch a singles tennis match. You will see the match being played in the minds of the two players. Sooner or later, one will become more confident and Positive. The other will start to make mistakes. It may be that one of the players starts to think that luck and the linesmen are against her or him. Or it may be that one of them suddenly feels inspired, believing that she or he cannot make a mistake. The game is a flow of Positive and Negative, with Positive winning every time. You can often see the same thing happening if you watch a football or cricket match and more so in the many games of life.

The underlying idea is summarised in Henry Ford's famous statement:

'Those who believe they can and those that believe they can't, are both right'

or by Hamlet's:

'There is nothing either good or bad but thinking makes it so'.

Affirmations

You can make positive affirmations or statements about yourself to enhance the image you have of yourself.. Write these on cards and repeat them as many times as possible during the day. Casius Clay's 'I am the greatest' is a good example.

I have terrific energy and focus' 'I have a wonderful wife, husband, child, parent, teacher etc.', 'I am very intelligent', 'I am very happy'. are examples, not necessarily true at the moment you write them and say them to yourself, but which express what you would like to happen. This is an old but very effective idea. A psychiatrist called Coue was one of the pioneers of positive thinking and recommended that you say twenty times every day 'Every day and in every way, I am getting better and better' Reading the biographies of the famous and successful will reveal that many of them achieved fame using this approach. If you are feeling miserable, try the 'I am very happy' affirmation and smile every time you look in a mirror. It is most surprising how well this works. Equally important is to avoid negative thoughts. Kill them off as soon as you become aware of them. And watch out for them.

If you are a singer, you might repeatedly tell yourself that you are highly talented, greatly admired and successful. You visualise yourself on the stage, causing the audience to experience joy and rapture at your performance. You hear their applause which you graciously acknowledge. You see the adulation of critics in the papers. This is almost certainly better than encouraging the Negative by believing that you are not all that good, in danger of forgetting the notes and the words and having visions of boos and cat calls when you perform This 'seeing' it, is an important part of the technique. Avoid seeing the Negative but think about the Positive things you want to do as though they had already come to pass.

Prescriptions

Do not feel guilty about your ambitions. Realise that there is abundance in this world and that you do not need to achieve your ambitions at the expense of others.

You will see what you look for. If you look Negatively, you will find problems and difficulties. If you look Positively, you will find opportunities and solutions. You are either learning and growing or going downhill. It is by doing that you learn.

View failures objectively, as providing information from which you can learn. To repeat, the seeds of many successful enterprises have been sown in the soil of failures.

Eliminate 'can't' and 'impossible' from your vocabulary. Examine carefully what you consider limits or constrains you. Are they real or just 'cop-outs'? Might they just be mirages which will disappear as you approach them? Can you see ways round them or are they a source of comfort and security?

A few more Positive thinking ideas

*   It is evident, in theory at any rate, that you can control yourself, impose self-discipline and walk with pride. You need never accept less than the best for yourself. In practice, it is not easy to achieve this desirable state and there are many gurus, cults and techniques making fortunes by helping people to do this.

*   However, the secret is simple - TAKE ACTION. No techniques, no mumbo-jumbo - JUST TAKE ACTION. Just think about it and concentrate on this simple instruction. Make a start, push out the boat, let the wind fill the sails. TAKE ACTION NOW. It is all a matter of will power.

*   This belief that you can be free comes from abandoning the idea that something is controlling you. Fear needs to be replaced by love - of life, of people, of yourself and of Creation.

*   A Frenchman, Jean de la Fontaine' writing in the 17th, Century said 'Help yourself and heaven will help you.' As someone else said 'God helps those who help themselves.'

List the good Positive things that you value and the Negative things you dislike. This can often be surprisingly revealing. Then it is also often reassuring to list all the Positive things that are happening around you, such as gains, wins, good luck, learning, growth. Finally, if you feel you are not sufficiently Positive, try making a list of the actions you are going to take to become more Positive - such as repeating Positive affirmations daily, refusing to entertain Negative thoughts and attitudes, doing everything as well as possible. The Self Counselling questions that follow will help you to counsel yourself to be Positive and eliminate the Negative. If you do nothing else this has the potential to have a profound effect on your life for the better.

Self Counselling No. 4.1 Positive and Negative

In general in life, think of and list the good Positive things you value

In general in life, think of and list the Negative things you dislike

In your personal life, what Positive things are happening around you e.g. gains, good luck, learning, growth. agreements etc.?

In the relationships you already have, think about and list what Positive aspects, qualities, capabilities each person has.

In your personal life, what Negative things are happening around you e.g. losses, bad luck, mistakes, failures, disagreements etc.?

In the relationships you already have, think about and list what Negative aspects, traits each person has.

Your experience

almost always	very often	fairly often	50% of the time	not very often	seldom	almost never

*How much of the time do
you feel Positive?*

*How much of the time do
you feel Negative?*

*Think of and list the actions you are going to take to become more Positive and
less Negative. Complete the results column in 4 weeks time and then list further
actions as necessary.*

ACTIONS   *RESULTS FOUR WEEKS LATER*

Self Counselling No.4.2 Assumptions

Before you start to interact with someone or whilst you are doing so, it is useful to check the assumptions you are making. Tick POSITIVE OR NEGATIVE for each assumption below, for an important relationshjp you are developing. Repeat the exercise for any other important relationships.

Name.................

MY ASSUMPTIONS - What you think is your position –
POSITIVE OR NEGATIVE
What you think is her/his position –
POSITIVE OR NEGATIVE

HER/HIS ASSUMPTIONS -   What you think he/she thinks her/his
position is – POSITIVE OR NEGATIVE
What do you think she/he thinks your
position is – POSITIVE OR NEGATIVE

Do you need to change these assumptions and if so how are you going to do it?

Name.................

MY ASSUMPTIONS - What you think is your position –
        POSITIVE OR NEGATIVE
        What you think is her/his position –
        POSITIVE OR NEGATIVE

HER/HIS ASSUMPTIONS -   What you think he/she thinks her/his
        position is – POSITIVE OR NEGATIVE
        What do you think she/he thinks your
        position is – POSITIVE OR NEGATIVE

Do you need to change these assumptions and if so how are you going to do it?

Name.................

MY ASSUMPTIONS - What you think is your position –
        POSITIVE OR NEGATIVE
        What you think is her/his position –
        POSITIVE OR NEGATIVE

HER/HIS ASSUMPTIONS -   What you think he/she thinks her/his
        position is – POSITIVE OR NEGATIVE
        What do you think she/he thinks your
        position is – POSITIVE OR NEGATIVE

Do you need to change these assumptions and if so how are you going to do it?

Self Counselling No.4.3 Affirmations

Think about and write down a number of positive affirmations declaring the goals you desire to achieve as if they are already achieved and happening now.

For example 'I am a millionaire. I have a wonderful Mercedes, a house in the country, a yacht on the Hamble'.
or
'I am helping the children in Mozambique to be educated. I am collecting funding from every direction. I am going to Mozambique to make a difference.'

Now write your own. You might start with;

'Every day and in every way I am getting better and better. I am very successful and. I never think of failure or limitations.' Now continue on with your own affirmations

The next Chapter 5 provides you with a simple model of the human being in terms of mind, body, spirit and the way these elements within a person communicate with each other and with the same elements in another person. This is exciting material and gives you a tremendous advantage in understanding yourself and others better, as you pursue your goals

CHAPTER 5

HOW TO TALK TO YOURSELF AND TO OTHERS THROUGH THE FIVE ELEMENTS OF A PERSON

A SIMPLE MODEL OF THE HUMAN BEING

'The proper study of mankind is man' - Pope

Why do we need a model?

.If you want to know how to make things happen the way you want, it is useful to try to understand who you are, and how you communicate with yourself and with others. There are many things about being human that we do not really understand, so we have to pretend to know. For example, we do not know what we are doing here on this bit of cosmic dust in a vast Universe. We don't know what happens when we die. So we invent explanations. The human being is incredibly complex and, in many respects, a mystery. To talk about aspects useful to the understanding of how people interact, it is helpful to simplify and construct a model.

A psychological model attempts to explain what something is like in such a way that it will enable predictions to be made of what will happen, if certain things are done or come about. Such models are a form of science fiction because they are not exact replicas of reality. If the reality were known, there would be no need for a model. But if a model explains what is happening and allows predictions to be made with a fair degree of accuracy, then it can be very useful.

The concept of mind, body and spirit, which is such a model, is now widely accepted. These three elements of the human being communicate between themselves and with the Positive and Negative discussed in Chapter 4. All of these elements are known to you and I through experience.

The spirit

In every person, there is something or someone 'looking' or capable of 'looking' at the body, what it is doing and at what the mind thinks. It is impossible to find anything material that represents this 'me' but it is undoubtedly as 'real' as the table from which one eats.

'And I said to myself, it's a wonderful world'. Satchmo

Every human is a spiritual being, and this is the entity that you recognise as being yourself and which is separate from your mind and body. It is necessary to distinguish between you, the whole person, consisting of the spirit, mind and body on the one hand, and on the other, the spirit alone, which I will indicate in bold lettering as **you**. **You** are an entity, a phenomena, who is aware that **you** are a spirit separate from the physical body and the mind. After all, **you** can look at what *your* body is doing and similarly at what *your* mind is thinking. **You** can partially - but probably, not completely - control both *your* body and *your* mind. **You** are a prisoner of *your* body but not of *your* mind. (Some people would dispute this and believe that it is possible to move your spiritual self outside of your body.) The spiritual **you** which does these things is non-material. It cannot be seen any more than the wind can, but what **you** do can be very evident.

Who has seen the wind
Neither you nor I,
But when the trees bow down their heads,
The wind is passing by

The mind

We think of the mind as being in the brain. It is an astonishing and miraculous entity with a capability of thinking that far exceeds that of any computer. It has a memory with massive storage and the ability to imagine, have ideas, invent patterns and pictures. No one knows where these come from, whether from within the mind or from outside. **You** are in almost constant communication with it and it, with **you**. It talks to **you** almost incessantly - sometimes **you** are listening and sometimes not. **You** give it instructions, ask it to do various things, some simple and others complex and *you* look at what it has produced. It is difficult to believe that what seems like a small lump of organic matter can have such fantastic miraculous capability.

The body

The body is an awesome apparatus with a plethora of built-in computers, controlling many of its functions. Often it seems to have a mind of its own. The body has feelings - some unwanted, some pleasurable. The sources of some are obvious - a nice meal, a wonderful play, an accident - but some just settle, like a flock of vultures, for no good reason. You can feel miserable at a party or lonely in a crowd. Feelings produce physical, bodily reactions such as laughter, tears, sweating, sexual response - and these often reinforce the feelings.

Your body can have headaches, wheezes, sneezes, itches for no apparent reason, or it can have disorders and diseases, some of which are explicable and often curable, and some are not. It is capable of two-way communication with other people's bodies - the so-called body language.

The Positive

The Positive is the plus element in every person and, as has been outlined in Chapter 4, is good, honest, listening and acknowledging, understanding, seeking agreement, liking, loving, successful, enthusiastic, disciplined and ordered, unselfish, beautiful, secure. It magnifies and praises. It is the sunshine of life, the bliss everyone craves. The Positive can invade the person in a variety of ways. An external event may do the trick - a lovely day, a beautiful piece of music, a win, love. *You* can cause the Positive to appear by a wish, a strong desire that something good should happen. A continuous injection of Positive thoughts, wishes, intentions, desires by *you* into *your* consciousness causes the Positive to appear and sometimes make the desired things happen.

The Negative

The Negative is the minus element such as bad, dishonest, not listening, ignoring, seeking disagreement, disliking, hating, failing, apathetic, being undisciplined, disordered and selfish, belittling, criticising, ugly, insecure, brutal and sadistic. We are all conscious of the Negative in ourselves to some extent but, for most of us, possibly not conscious enough. Most of us have skeletons in the cupboard. Jung, the famous psychoanalyst, thought it preferable to take the skeletons out and dust them rather than shut the door firmly on them. The Negative is a destructive force, *your* enemy, and to borrow from a famous book, perhaps *your* executioner and the cause of psychosomatic illnesses. It is the force that causes panic when clear minds and courage are required. If a fire breaks out in a theatre, many of those who lose their lives are trampled to death by those in terror and possessed by their Negative.

Some emotions may sometimes be appropriate but they can also be Negative, and more harmful than beneficial.

Communication between you, the mind, the body, the Positive and the Negative

Most of the skills, principles and techniques of communicating, which are described in the next Chapter, apply to the internal communications between the five elements of the human being.

You and your mind

When *you* talk, *you* are communicating with the mind, which, in turn, is communicating with the body. *You* can instruct it to solve problems, remember words, concepts, happenings. *You* can bring things out of the memory, pluck ideas from outer space, imagine and invent, conjure up thoughts and pictures with the help of the mind and store them back in the memory again. *You* have the capability of separating yourself from the mind, of looking at what it is saying and of passing judgment

The relationship *you* have with the mind is something built up, over a lifetime. It is a two-way relationship. *You* exercise total control in carrying out many everyday tasks. However, more often than not, what occurs is influence or partial control. For example, sometimes *you* can make the mind do what you want but sometimes it will fail to remember or recall something you know very well that it knows. Sometimes it is difficult to know if it is *you* that is thinking and talking or is it the mind in auto-pilot.? It is like driving a car, when for a great deal of the time it is driven without *you* being in control. Hopefully whatever drives the car alerts *you* when anything untoward happens. Similarly, when *you* are talking there is an interplay between the mind working on its own and *your* intervention and control. Sometimes you cannot control what the mind instructs the voice to say - you say something *you* didn't intend to say.

There is a constant two-way communication between *you* and *your* mind and a constant interplay of influence and control. Thoughts come into your mind which can have a profound effect on you - thoughts of fear, loneliness, abandonment, envy, are just a few of what we call disturbing and Negative thoughts. But you also have the capability of not letting them have any effect on you. The mind speaks to *you* a great deal of the time, without *you* necessarily wanting it to do so. It is a great natterer like someone who can't stop talking. If *you* want it to shut up, it can prove difficult to get it to do so. Sometimes it stops you going to sleep. The chatter can be Positive but all too frequently, it is Negative and downbeat, and you need to be able to put it in a box and close the lid.

You and your body

You can look at the body and make it do things. The relationship and control *you* have over *your* body can be total in some situations. For example, a pianist can achieve such control that all the notes can be struck exactly as the pianist wishes. However, to a considerable extent, *you* influence the body rather than control it - sometimes you get it to do what you want and sometimes you don't. For example, if *you* have decided to lose weight, sometimes you will have the will to refuse a cake with your coffee and sometimes you won't.

The body can therefore communicate with you directly without the intervention of the mind. You can cease to be separate from the body but can become part of it, entangled with it, if it is in pain or is experiencing emotion. No longer are *you* in control - the body has assumed control over *you*.

As a spiritual being, *you* can convey spirit through the body, for example, by the touch of a musician or a lover, the physical skill of an artist, the body of a dancer but also in many ways during the daily activities of ordinary life. This is a priceless ability which can enhance everything you do. It is perhaps what is meant by grace.

You and the Positive and the Negative

It is often said of somebody that she/he is in high spirits. The Positive can make this happen. Being in love, passing an examination, seeing a beautiful flower - all such Positive external happenings can increases *your* awareness of *your* spirituality and ability to be separate from *your* mind and body.

The other side of the coin is that it can also be said of someone that she/he is dispirited. This can be brought about by the Negative. Death, loss, an accident, a criticism - all such Negative happenings can reduce *your* awareness of *your* spirituality and *you* can become identified with *your* body in such a way that *you* lose control over *your* Negative feelings and bodily reactions. *You* seem to become, for example, anxious, depressed, belligerent. Also, it is likely that *your* mind will be adversely affected because you may have forfeited influence over it, so that it is prone to make incorrect decisions.

Communication between the mind, body, Positive and Negative

The mind and the body

The two-way communication between body and mind is evident in any physical activity. The interplay can also be psychological. For example, if you are worried about an examination or when on a busy motorway, thoughts of insecurity can produce physical symptoms - an increased heart beat, possibly accompanied by emotions such as fear and panic. Thoughts can promote action, positively such as making love or negatively such as running wildly away. The other way round, the body can cause the mind to have thoughts - for example, physical sexual feelings can cause the mind to imagine erotic situations, and pains can foster thought of illness.

Emotions are feelings which often seem to appear and disappear without *your* control. They may be produced by thought or memory but are often spontaneous reactions to the messages coming into the body. It would appear that a normal, reasonable level of emotions is programmed into most individuals to serve a protective or life enhancing purpose. In a way they seem like special keys on a computer, which when pressed set a routine in motion. Some buttons are Positive and some Negative. The Negative ones are often excessive and uncontrollable. Sometimes they are chronic such as depression or obsessions. They have the ability to entangle the mind and the spirit so that illogical and destructive actions take place which in extreme cases can lead to such calamities as accidents, manslaughter, murder and suicide.

There is evidence that physical pain can be experienced that emanates not from the body but from the mind. The view is widespread that the mind and the words it uses can have a profound effect on the immune system of the body and can affect, for good or bad, the health and well-being of the individual. However, lack of emotions or emotional response can communicate a Negative message to a person who is highly emotional.

Many people are not in accord or in good communication with their bodies. This is very evident to speech therapists who have to try to establish a better relationship between mind and body, to effect cures. It is also relevant to trainers in sports. Many very physical games are won in the minds of the competitors.

The mind and the Positive and the Negative

A mind which is in communication with the Positive has Positive thoughts and this generally makes it more capable of creativity, clear thinking and of solving problems. The mind can generate Positive thoughts and ideas and can also interpret messages received from outside in a Positive way,- with *your* encouragement but often of its own volition. The need to think Positively to achieve success, power and serenity is evident.

A mind in communication with the Negative has Negative thoughts and its ability to think clearly is likely to be impaired. Just as with Positive thoughts, the mind can generate Negative ones and interpret what happens Negatively. Such thoughts generally produce emotional reactions and stress. It is often difficult for *you* to stop it doing so, unless *you* are aware of what is happening and can separate *yourself* from the Negativity.

Communication between the body and the Positive and the Negative

In communication with the Positive, the body can be fit, strong and feel good and energetic. It can have a confident carriage. It can be skilful. It can convey positive attitudes and feelings and can seek and absorb Positive images and experiences. Sports coaches put great emphasis on the way Positive attitudes affect performance in athletics and physical games. Commentators on cricket matches increasingly have become aware of the body language of the players, particularly of the fielding side as a batsman dominates the game.

In communication with the Negative, the body can be unfit, obese, weak, and feel bad and fatigued. Negative body language is apparent in the carriage, facial expression and physical performance. For example, under pressure, a golfer can make wrong decisions, choose the wrong club and the wrong route to the next hole, and fail to achieve the physical skill demanded by the situation. The very experienced professional golfer learns how to avoid the pressure getting to her/him. The body can convey Negative attitudes and feelings, which can stimulate Negative attitudes in others. It can also seek and absorb Negative images and experience.

Communication between the Positive and the Negative

The Positive can overcome the Negative, if it can be mustered when the Negative is holding sway. *You* and the mind can generate Positive thoughts that can push the Negative out of the system. This is easier said than done and although possible for most people, it seems to be extremely difficult, if not impossible, for those suffering from acute depression.

To summarise

Messages are passing to and fro between *you*, mind, body and the Positive and the Negative all the time that *you* are awake. Meditation is a technique used to stop these flows and is a good way to become aware of your spiritual self.

The key concept is the separation of *you*, from mind, body, Positive and Negative, because this puts *you* in control.

Communication between the five elements of two persons

When you and I are communicating, all the interplay between the five elements - spirit, mind, body, Positive and Negative - is taking place within both of us and between us. Our bodies communicate directly with each other. So do our minds and, when, for example, we are in love, so do our spirits. Positive will communicate with Positive and Negative with Negative. The amount of activity that is going on at any time is prodigious and it is not surprising that communication between two people is not simple. If *you* can become increasingly aware of this activity, *you* can become like a conductor of an orchestra and the composer of the music.

In the following passage some of these interactions are evident.

He saw her come over the hill. He was immediately aware of the beauty of her figure. His body was already reacting. His mind was counselling caution.

She felt apprehensive when she saw him. He was obviously going to pass close. Should she acknowledge him as he came towards him or should she look the other way?

As he got closer, he seemed to be looking at her intently. She felt naked under his gaze.

He was aware that he could not stop looking at her, although his mind was telling him to look disinterested. He now realised he had seen her before. She worked in a flower shop in the town.

She thought she had seen him somewhere. She started to think about the newspaper reports of there being a rapist at large. She didn't usually take this short cut over the hill, along a lane with high banks. There was really nowhere to escape and he was coming closer.

'She shouldn't be out here alone' he thought. 'She is very vulnerable'.

As they approached, he called 'Good morning' and then 'Haven't we met somewhere?'

She was disconcerted and walked past. Then she felt guilty at being so unfriendly and turned round. He had also turned round to enjoy her departing figure. They both laughed. He opened his arms as if to say, 'Don't be afraid'.

She said 'I am sorry to be unfriendly but I really don't know who you are'.

He said 'I know who you are - you work in Timmins flower shop. I'm Joe Collins and I'm a vet on my way to Hill Top Farm. I thought I would take some exercise as it is such a fine morning'.

She said 'I must go now. I'm due at the flower shop in five minutes' and she turned and walked on down the hill, feeling as if he was looking after her, not wanting to turn round, but after a moment or two, she couldn't stop herself doing so and, yes, he was standing in an attitude of admiration and he blew her a kiss,

She waved and turned to walk back into town feeling strangely elated.

Self Counselling No 5.1 Communication with your internal family.

This questionnaire is designed to help you think about your own communication with your internal 'family', your body, mind and Positive and Negative elements. From this analysis, think about and list the communications you wish to make with your 'family', e.g to stop smoking with your body, to learn Spanish with your mind, to send your Negative to Coventry, to ask your Positive to help you achieve your goals.

As to your body:

Is it fit and healthy?　　*If not, what ailments?*

Does it smoke?　　*Does it drink alcohol?*　　*Does it take drugs?*

Does it eat excessively?　　*Does it have any other bad habits?*

Do you intend to do anything about these - if 'yes', what?

*How much of the time do **you** control your body?*

What do you do with it? e.g. walk. play hockey, exercise etc,

As to your mind

Has it a good memory?   How often does it give you the right answer

How much of the time does it communicate with the Positive?

How much of the time does it communicate with the Negative?

Is it imaginative?   What do you do with it e.g. write, paint, run a factory

As to your Negative

How often does it control you?
How often does it control your mind?
How often does it control your body?
Do you encourage it or positively refuse to have anything to do with it?

As to your Positive

How often does it control you?
How often does it control your mind?
How often does it control your body?
Do you communicate with and have a good relationship with the Positive?

Any actions? If 'yes', list below.

CHAPTER 6

THE SECRETS OF SUCCESSFUL PERSON-TO-PERSON COMMUNICATION

'All the world's a stage
And all the men and women merely players
… One man in his time plays many parts'
'As you like it'- Shakespeare

This Chapter is concerned with tactics, planning, techniques - what many books refer to as 'secrets' or 'magic', but what is mostly common sense. All you have to do is to try the various ideas out, see which work for you and do the self counselling to clarify your ideas and to review your progress.

Who do you need to contact?

If you have developed the action lists recommended in Chapter 3, there will be a number of people you need to make contact with, if you have not already done so. When you made up your list, how ambitious were you? Did you reject some names because you feared a rebuff? This is understandable if you did, but it is important to reject any Negative thoughts that might limit you. You need to aim for the top. This is easier to do as a planning exercise on paper, when you can dream of engaging the help of people who are already successes.

When the time comes to move to reality, to pick up the telephone, it may well seem as if you are attempting the impossible. If there is one message that this book is determined to get across, it is that faith will move mountains and that confidence is the magic ingredient of success. Lack of confidence is the enemy of successful communication and can be a major factor preventing you from initiating a communication in the first place. The worst that can happen in most communications, however ambitious, is rejection, being turned down, getting a blunt 'No!' People of influence or importance are still only people like you and I.

AGC - Action or Agreement Generating Communication

When I talk about communication, I am talking about communication which is intended to initiate action or at least, initiate agreement that will result in action. For shorthand, I use the letters AGC - action generating or agreement generating communication. So if I talk to you and you are unaffected I would say that no communication has taken place. But AGC may be, and often is, partially effective. Some actions and agreement may be generated but only a proportion of the total which was intended. Also unintended results may be obtained. For example, you may be teaching me to drive a car and giving an explanation of how the clutch works. This may confuse rather than help me and so I might become emotional and less able to cope with the task.

In person-to-person communication, it is surprising how often people have messages they are afraid will be met with a Negative response and so really do not want the other person to receive. Possibly they will want to say at a later date 'I told you so' but they hope that the other person does not really take the message aboard. This often explains the reluctance to put things clearly in writing, the use of professional jargon and the 'small print'. 'If you look carefully you will see that it says, 'I did tell you, but you obviously weren't listening'.
.
Experience and research suggests that in person-to-person verbal communication, only 60% of a complicated message is understood even if the communicating is done well. Clearly the accuracy of a message passed through several people can deteriorate rapidly. The efficiency of written communication is often less because people often do not read what is put in front of them.

Another reason why some communication is ineffective is because the person initiating the communication is confused about what she/he wants to happen as a result. If this is so, what will be communicated to the other person will be her/his confusion and indecision.

Be a salesperson

So we are concerned with AGC (action/agreement generating communication), not just social chat. We can most simply think of it being between a seller and a customer. I qualified as a Civil Engineer but in one of my first jobs I found myself working for the Sales Director in Technical Service. He told me I had to sell. I remonstrated that I had not studied to take an honours degree, only to finish up as a salesman. He said 'You will have to learn to sell, if you are going to get anywhere'. The message gradually got through to me, that whenever one is trying to influence and convince someone, one is selling and that it is one of the most important skills in life. When you are the initiator of AGC, (the AGCer) you are the salesperson.

What? Where? When? Where? How?

What do you have to do to make a successful action generating communication (AGC) to the person receiving, i.e. the customer? Firstly you have to get her/his attention and get her/him to listen to you. Next, before you start, you have to think through: What? Where? When? Where? How? Let's assume you are going to make an AGC to me.

What? - decide what you want to happen. Be clear what you want me to do.

Who? - decide on the people with whom you have to communicate. In this instance you think your objective can best be achieved by talking to me. The reason you have chosen me is because you think I can take the action you want or because you think I am the most easily influenced person or the one with the best understanding and experience.

When? - When will I be in the most receptive mood? If I am a buyer, avoid times when you know I will be dealing with mail or attending regular management meetings. Why not ask my secretary or assistant. If I am a housewife, then it may be best to talk after the children have been put to bed. Whoever I am, choose a time when I am going to be relaxed and not interrupted. Timing is very important.

Where? Decide the 'stage' for the communication - e.g. the pub, office, club, restaurant.

The 'stage' is, in itself, a message. I have negotiated pay deals very successfully in a pub and sold consultancy in Board Rooms. The wrong stage can be disastrous. Generally, a restaurant or a sporting event are good places to make an arrangement to meet to discuss whatever it is you want to get across but not actually to have the discussion itself. This is best done in a quiet place, where there is little likelihood of interruptions. However, if you find yourself in front of someone who is constantly interrupted by telephone calls, you may think the local pub to be the better of two evils as far as communication is concerned.

How? - do you try to talk on a one-to-one basis or would you like to have someone with you. Professional salesmen often prefer the latter, so that one can talk and the other listen. Generally face-to-face is best, without anything - like a desk or table - in between. AGC in a car is generally difficult.. There is little eye contact. The driver cannot give all of his attention and may feel captive if the passenger is too forceful. I remember only too well that I once endangered my job by complaining to my boss when he was driving and I was sitting beside him.

The message

The message has to be clear and concise to motivate someone to take action. It has to have regard to anything that has gone before. It needs to avoid causing Negative emotion or irrationality. It should be conveyed with enthusiasm, energy and vitality. If you are nervous, it is all too easy to talk about anything but what really matters. If you are not careful your resolve can fail and you can come away from a discussion with nothing.

The message has to get the agreement of someone to do something, whether this is by reasoned argument or by threats of coercion or both. For example 'I will put the facts to her but if she doesn't see reason, I will point out that the law is on my side and I might prosecute'. The assessment of the nature and strength of relationships is important in achieving successful communication and this is further considered in Chapter 7.

Getting the message across

This phrase implies projecting a message from the talker to the listener. In person-to-person communication, this means conveying conviction, a very positive desire to achieve a result, a Positive belief in the truth and importance of what is being put across. If you have a very strong will to succeed, this will be evident in all aspects of your communication - not only the words but your facial expression, body language, and manner of speaking. But you must avoid talking too much, conveying stress and anxiousness. Again it is not unlike what a good golfer has to do - tee the ball up, select the right club, have regard to wind and terrain, judge distance and direction, swing back the club, keep head still, start the down swing. Finally he has to hit the ball hard and true in just the right spot and get it across to exactly where he wants it to be. Get your powerful message across and then say no more, until you see whether it has landed.

Check these important things-to-do

In a communication between you and someone else – say me:

1. Get my attention and willingness to listen to you. If you don't seem to be able to achieve this, it may be because I've something important on my mind. You may have to do a good deal of listening and adopt a counselling role, before you can start to get your message across.
2. Talk to yourself Positively until you are in a relaxed and confident mood, and optimistic about the outcome.
3. Avoid being aggressive, so don't start trying to talk if you are angry. You will only convey anger.
4. Try not to talk if you are afraid or cast down. As with anger, all you will do is to communicate your fear, sadness or self-pity.
5. Feel happy about the exchange of views you are undertaking and let this be evident
6. Listen and let me do most of the talking. Acknowledge what I say from time to time with murmurs of agreement and approval, if you can do so honestly.
7. Never assume that you know what I am thinking or going to say.
8. Find out what I really want.
9. Talk to me in such a way that I am in a relaxed mood - but don't lose sight of what you want to achieve.
10. Approach me with genuine regard and concern. Find something to admire about me – appearance, accomplishments, good judgement, for example..
11. Be yourself and give all your attention to the communication.
12. Observe my reactions. If these are different from what you want to happen, note the difference and seek an explanation. Afterwards, write this down so that you can build up a diary of experience from which

you can learn.

13. Try to achieve eye contact - but do not overdo it.
14. Make yourself feel that I am important and project this feeling. Build up my self esteem.
15. Make sure you understand what I am saying.
16. Be impressed by me. Be interested and ask questions.
17. Talk with conviction but avoid too loud a voice or overbearing a manner.
18. Try to get my agreement to hear you out and to understand what it is you are trying to put across.
19. Try to ensure that you have plenty of time, otherwise you may give the wrong impression of being impatient or in too much of a hurry.
20. Be capable of apologising if you behave unreasonably and of admitting you are wrong, if you are
21. 'The medium is the message' is a message from the 60's. It means that the medium you use to communicate with, is a message in itself. Examples are: A crumpled piece of paper. 'He took the trouble to speak to me personally', 'Good news always comes verbally but bad news in writing', 'We were impressed by the trouble he had taken with the diagrams'

An interplay of ideas

Effective communication involves an interplay of ideas. It is quite different from an argument. Whoever is talking is in control, because the listener should be giving her/him all her/his attention, trying to understand what is being said and letting the talker know 'message received and understood'. The role of talker and listener has to be exchanged until, hopefully, agreement is reached. In negotiations, when there has been a good deal of conflict, I have found it useful to get it agreed that in one session, one party will talk and the other party listen and only ask questions to make sure that everything is thoroughly understood. The listening party can then go away and analyse and think about what was said and prepare for the next meeting when he/she or they can be heard without interruption. A succession of meetings of this sort can often bring about a successful conclusion. It avoids the aggression that can arise from interruptions and disagreements.

It is generally unnecessary to meet every argument with a counter argument. It is possible to get the feeling that if you do not deal with something you disagree with right away, the opportunity to do so will be lost. Actually, people rarely listen to you when you do this. But usually, there is always another day when you can get your disagreement heard and possibly eventually reach agreement.

The 'here and now'

The ability to get into and stay in the 'here-and-now' is a skill that is worth learning and practicing. It is a process of controlling the mind, rejecting extraneous thoughts about somewhere else or some other time, focusing on what you want to get across. It is the ability exhibited by a golfer making a long putt on the 18th green, when getting the ball in the hole will secure the championship and a great deal of money. Thoughts of failure, what to do with the money, of what the spectators think, what the TV camera can see, of the acclamation that success will bring, have all to be absent from the golfer's mind. It is just her/him, here and now, with the ball and the hole, her/his muscles, and stance and eye.

Make a start on this by seeing how long you can stay in the 'here and now' and practice this vital ability.

Making the customer comfortable

The initial conversation should create a pleasant atmosphere. Assuming you are the salesperson and I am the customer, initiate a conversation that is not AGC but just something agreeable. You might ask about my family, recent holidays, the football or cricket team I follow. You try to find something to admire about me and let me know you do so. You ask my opinion about something. You try to make sure I am not worrying about anything and that I am in the 'here-and-now'.

Getting attention

If you want to achieve AGC with me, it is absolutely essential to get my full attention before you do anything else. You must make sure that I am ready and willing to receive, to be on the same wavelength and listening. To achieve this, I have to have a good reason for wanting to listen to you. If this does not exist, you have to provide it. One way of doing this is to make an arresting statement, to say something that is so important to me or that is so exceptional that I am 'all ears'. Another way is to discuss the reason for the communication and to establish why it is so important for me to listen.

If you have not got my attention after having made some efforts to do so, it may well be that I have some other very important thing on my mind. You need to be sensitive to this possibility. You might even ask 'Have you something on your mind that is worrying you? Would you rather deal with that first and then talk again when you have sorted it out?' You can't always assume that I am a blank piece of paper with an open uncluttered mind ready to receive your message.

Reactions

An important skill in communicating is being acutely aware of what is happening to the person to whom you are talking. It is relatively easy to see if she/he is getting angry - red in the face - or tearful - crying - agitated - walking about. Peoples' gestures and body language can also disclose much information. Does the other person make eye contact? Does she/he blink a lot? Does she/he yawn, look bored. Physical appearance and how you say it is often more important that what you say. People often buy salesmen rather than the product.

Things not to do :

* Say or infer 'You are wrong'.
* Say 'No'. Rather, say 'Possibly' even if you would like to say 'No'.
* Argue.
* Offer unasked-for opinions.
* Knock the competition.
* Assume authority.
* Oversell and talk too much.
* Interrupt.
* Disagree, unless absolutely necessary.
* Try to win an argument

To recap

The selling type communication, in which you have to engage if you are going to persuade someone to buy - not necessarily a product, but, for example, an idea or a principle - starts with creating a warm, pleasant atmosphere, with positive feelings towards the person to whom you are selling, continues with questions rather than statements, leads to establishing needs and requirements, overcoming objections and then when the time is right, to the message, to what salesmen call 'the close'. Do try to ensure clarity as to what you have agreed. Once this has been done, exit as speedily as possible.

Honesty

It is essential to be honest if you are going to gain anyone's confidence. There is a magic in complete frankness and openness. Dishonesty kills the possibility of successful communication, because it means that it is impossible to separate lies from the truth and so nothing can be believed.

Mental attitude and rapport

Anyone is free to assume a mental attitude which will attract and please others, or repel and antagonise them. This is something quite apart from words or body language. It is important to achieve rapport and sympathy with me. One way of doing this is to share the same small talk in terms of my interests, if this is possible - for example - schools, children, gardening, football, cars, clothes. The most fundamental interest of anyone is her/himself. You can try to be comfortable with my gestures and body language.

Being in accord at an emotional level may also help in achieving rapport but sometimes this may be disadvantageous, because it can sometimes be more helpful to maintain an objective viewpoint and avoid the risk of becoming entangled emotionally.

Also remember that some people often think in terms of one of three senses - seeing, hearing and feeling - pictures, sounds (words), and feelings. When you are talking with me, if you can discover in which of these three modes I am thinking, you can modify your own communications to express your ideas in the same mode.

One way is to listen to spoken clues.

If I'm thinking in terms of sounds I might say
'I hear what you say'
'I don't like the sound of that'
'He is just a big mouth'

If I'm thinking in terms of pictures I may say
'Look! This is important'

'I can see what you are getting at'
'Your meaning is obscure'.

If I'm thinking in terms of feeling and touch I may say
'We will be in touch'
'I don't feel that is right'
'Hold on!'.

Does the message hit the target?

The golfer can observe whether the ball goes where he wants it to go but the communicator cannot always do so. It would be nice if you could get back 'message received and understood', better still 'message received and agreed with'. What you can aim to do is to say or infer something like 'Just hear me out, listen to what I have to say, make sure there is nothing you don't understand and let me know when you have taken it aboard. Then I will do the same for you'.

How language works

Speed

The speed with which you talk conveys a message; for example, whether you are nervous or confidant, reasonable or arrogant. It is also important to leave pauses and to know when to shut up. Nervousness can cause you not to have the confidence to leave a space. This has the effect on me that I don't or can't say anything, and this causes you to feel under an obligation to go on talking.

Emphasis

The meaning of a sentence can depend on the emphasis that is put on the words. For example, in the sentence 'I am sure she was misleading me', try emphasising each word in turn - '<u>I</u> am sure...' - meaning, 'you may not be but I am'. 'I am <u>sure</u>...' meaning ''There is no doubt about it'. 'I am sure <u>she</u>...' - meaning 'Not anyone else'.' I am sure she <u>was</u>...' meaning 'but not any longer'. 'I am sure she was <u>misleading</u>...' - meaning 'Not telling me the truth'. 'I am sure she was misleading <u>me</u>' meaning 'And not anyone else'. It can be seen how easy it is for someone to hear a different emphasis from the one you think you have made and thus get a different message.

Loudness

Some people dominate by speaking very loudly whilst others can do the same by speaking very quietly so that you have to listen intently to what they are saying. You may have to speak louder to someone who is hard of hearing, but generally, a pleasantly modulated voice is most likely to please. People speak more loudly when they think they are not being heard, - they think they are not getting their message across and received. This loudness can be interpreted as irritation or anger and generally stimulates a loud response. Very soon a shouting match is going on, which is generally unproductive. However, variations in loudness and pitch can make a voice more interesting and persuasive.

Grammar and accent

Bad grammar, slang, and swearing convey a message, which may not be helpful to making a successful communication although in some situations it may establish rapport. However, it cannot be taken for granted that someone who uses strong language likes it being used by someone else. A few regional accents are generally regarded as attractive. Strong ones often make it difficult for someone outside of the region, to understand what is being said, but more temperate accents can often add character to someone's talk. None of these things necessarily affect the overall content of what is said.

Questions

Asking question and listening to the answers is a central theme of this book. However, it is important to appreciate that questions can readily be misinterpreted. 'When is supper going to be ready?' may be an innocent enquiry seeking information, perhaps to decide whether there is time to complete some task. It may be received as a complaint that preparing supper is taking a long time and evoke an appropriate reply. Often a question can sound like a criticism or being nosy or as a hint, so that it is essential to precede the question with some disarming and pleasant words so that it is received as intended.

The hidden message

Information is conveyed by the meaning of words. But the message between two people nearly always says something about the relationship. This is the 'hidden' message.

You say to me 'Please go and see Mr. Smith and see if you can get an order from him'

The messages I receive may be various.

The emphasis on 'please' suggests that you are irritated. 'But', you think 'Why should you be? I went to see Mr Smith only last month'.

See if you can get an order'. What would I be going to see Mr Smith about if it wasn't to get an order?' There is almost a suggestion of criticism for failure to get an order from Mr. Smith in the past.

But then there seemed to be an emphasis on 'you', as though others had also tried and failed.

The hidden message of a father explaining something to his twelve year old daughter, may be 'You are a bit thick and I'm cleverer than you' and to his wife, who is also listening, 'He is showing off again'. The outcome may be that the daughter looks bored and resentful and the wife says 'You are making it much too complicated', the hidden message of which is 'I wish you would stop'.

All the time people talk to each other, hidden messages are also being observed, exchanged and evaluated. Politician A, whose message is uninspiring, may put it over with a pleasant, disarming manner with the hidden message, 'I am a nice chap'. Politician B may be saying interesting and sensible things but in an unattractive and forceful way, when the hidden message is 'I am not a particularly nice chap'. So the average television viewer, who probably gives neither politician full attention, will tend to favour politician A.

It is always controversial to make generalisations about gender differences but it is possible that women are more interested in reading between the lines and more aware of hidden messages. This may be because they often have more intuitive understanding in relationships than men. The practical effect of this, particularly if you are a man, is that you should be aware of any hidden messages you may be conveying.

Legitimacy

It is reasonable to argue that it is legitimate to influence, persuade, to achieve compliance if both the means and ends are good. There are many occasions in everyday life when you can further your own ends without damaging those of others – so that everybody wins. But there are also many other situations where, if you win, someone else loses. This is all right if it is agreed that this is the way the game is set up. This includes, for example, most sports, buying and selling transactions and many legal negotiations.

However, there is enough recent history to be a warning that if the means and/or the ends are bad, it is possible for the legitimacy of influence and persuasion to be questionable and at worst, to be completely and unacceptably evil.

The skill of persuasion

The skilled persuader, say you, is intent on getting someone, say me, to do as you wish by achieving agreement. This implies that I see my best interest being served by doing what you want.

You have to control the conversation and eventually steer it towards what in sales jargon is known as 'the close'. This is the point at which the 'This is what I want you to do' message is put across. This is when the salesperson asks for the order.

However, the close message is not a straight 'Will you please do...' because this provides the opportunity for a negative reply. The close message is always a choice which already implies within it, acceptance of what you want me to do. 'Do you want the red or black one? 'Will you pay with cash or credit card?' Will you ask her this evening or tomorrow?'

You may use various motivators and these are discussed in Chapter 9. Basically, in the earlier stages of talking you try to discover my needs and if satisfying these does not seem sufficient for me to go along with what you want, then you have to suggest further needs to me i.e. benefits if I comply and losses if I don't.

What is sometimes called the 'chemistry' between two people, such as you and I, is very important. People often like or dislike someone at first sight. You have to be aware of this and if the chemistry is not right, you have to work hard to correct it. This may be achieved by identifying with me, trying to achieve empathy, and a sense of common purpose. In practice this means using the word 'we' As has already been said, it is no bad thing to find something to admire or appreciate about me and let me know you do so.

To summarise, you have to be a salesman if you are going to get anywhere. Start by creating a warm atmosphere, continue with questions rather than statements, establish needs and requirements and then, when the time is right, close. Once this is done, and hopefully a Positive acknowledgement and agreement has been obtained, exit as speedily as possible. Many a sale has been lost by letting the customer get off the hook. Once you have got agreement, try to cement it in whatever way seems appropriate - a document signed, money paid, a handshake, an agreed delivery date, location etc. All this has to have regard to whatever you are trying to sell.

The Communication Plan

This is a plan to carry out an important communication.

Firstly, decide on the preparatory comments that will establish a good atmosphere.

Next, list the questions most appropriate to ask to understand better the identity and the Positive or Negative assumptions of the person you are to communicate with and her/his points of view on the subject you want to communicate about.

List the persuasive points that you wish to control the conversation with and which will prepare for the close message.

List the expected objections and formulate answers that will not be arguments, that will not put the other person in the wrong but that will show sympathy for the objection, and take it aboard. These answers certainly require thought beforehand.

Finally, you decide how the final close message is to be put across.

All the above can be entered on Self Counselling 6.1 which follows.

Self Counselling 6.1 The Communication Plan

Communication No.   *Person(s) to be communicated with*

Result desired

Preparatory comment

Questions   *1*

                               2

                               3

The persuasive points   *1*

                               2

                               3

                               4

Expected objections   1
and answers

                        2

                        3

                        4

The close message

Self Counselling 6.2 Action List

This list states the actions you should take and the conditions you should attempt to achieve. It needs to be learnt by heart because you cannot take it with you.

Should be:

1. *Stage - seated, face to face, eye contact*

2. *Your feeling - relaxed, content, comfortable, alert*

3. *Your assumptions - I'm Positive, You're Positive – I am an Influencer (adult)*

4. *Her/his feeling - relaxed, content, comfortable*

5. *Her/his life assumptions - I'm Positive, You're Positive – I am an Influencer (adult)*

6. *Her/his attention - in the here and now - and on what I am saying*

7. *Your will to succeed - very strong desire*

8. *You express praise or admiration*

9. *You have love in your heart and you project it mentally*

10. *You project your message across*

11. *You achieve rapport and mutual liking*

12. *You get her/his acknowledgement*

13. *You listen attentively to her/his replies*

14. *You understand her/his point of view*

15. *You acknowledge effectively - message received and understood*

16. *You project Positive feelings and emotions*

17. *You signal an open, Positive attitude with your body language*

18. *You do not argue*

19. *You avoid disagreement*

20. *You avoid projecting an identity*

21. *How are you going to close?*

Self Counselling 6.3 What Happened? The Communication Action Report

1. How did you arrange the stage?

2. Did you sit face-to-face?

3. How much eye contact?

4. How did you feel e.g. relaxed, uncomfortable, enthusiastic etc.

5. What were your assumptions about yourself and the other person - Positive or Negative?

6. How strong was your will to succeed?

7. How did you feel she/he felt?

8. What did you think her/his assumptions were about her/himself and you – Positive or Negative?

9. Did she/he have attention elsewhere?

10. Did you find out and deal with it?

11. Did you get her/his attention finally?

12., Were you in the here and now?

13, Was she/he in the here and now?

14. Did you find something to praise?

15. Did you achieve an early rapport or mutual liking?

16. Did you get your message across?

17. Did you get your acknowledgements across?

18. Did she/he acknowledge?

19. Did you listen attentively?

20. *Did you understand her/his point of view?*

21. *Any emotions?*
    ME............................ HER/HIM.............................

22. *Any body signs?*
    ME............................ HER/HIM.............................

23. *Any silences?*
    ME .... HER/HIM.............................

24. *Any misunderstandings?*

25. *Any disagreements?*

26. *Did you talk too much?*

27. *Did you convey that you were listening attentively*

28 *How did you carry out the plans of Self Counselling 6.1*

29 *How did you close?*

30 *Result of the communication - Was the objective achieved? Was there any other result?*

Anything to learn from the above?

Every communication is a unique learning experience, if you choose to make it so. You do not want to think of failure. At least you can learn from it to discover what you did not do right and to formulate how you are going to avoid the errors in the next communication. In this way you will learn quickly.

Listening - Why it is important?

Most people spend much of their time listening - but it is mostly to themselves. When they are listening to someone else, they often take aboard about half of what is said to them and very soon after, only about a quarter is remembered. Listening is perhaps the most important activity in human communication. It is a skill that can be learnt and improved.

Not listening properly causes mistakes, misunderstandings, emotional reactions, and disagreement and can damage relationships. It is a cause of much waste of time and the source of many disputes. Patient, uninterrupted listening builds trust.

The only way to find out what is happening in human relationships is to listen. Unfortunately, people attempt to alter situations or solve human relation problems before they find out what is wrong, or how to put them right. It is like kicking, or rather not kicking, the television set if it is not working. The equivalent of taking the back off, looking carefully at the bits and pieces and connections, and making the necessary technical evaluation is, in human relations terms, to **ask questions and listen to the answers.** This simple, but little used technique has many good things going for it. If you ask enough questions and listen hard enough, you will generally discover where the trouble lies. Try to imagine that you have laryngitis and that you have lost your voice. You can just about manage to ask questions.

Listening to someone talking involves receiving messages, looking at and understanding them, keeping them in mind and conveying, if necessary, a response, 'message received and understood'.

Being listened to properly is a very rare experience. If you are not one already, try being a good listener. The results may astound you. It is very therapeutic for someone to be listened to. The person you listen to will warm to you and will be more prepared to hear what you have to say. If you are trying to solve a problem, by listening you can become more objective, separate yourself from the problem and become more effective in solving it.

Listening is part of the control agreement involved in communication. The listener, if giving full attention to the speaker, is being controlled - not in the sense of being forced to agree, but in the sense of being under the necessity of listening and understanding what is being said. To listen attentively is to inform the speaker that you have entered into the control agreement. It is often the way to start the ball rolling in a difficult situation.

What is involved in listening?

1. *Being interested in what the other person has to say and having an expectation that something of value will come across*
2. *Conveying to the talker that you are interested and want to hear the answer*
3. *Elimination from your mind of:*
   - *extraneous thoughts,*
   - *negative emotions,*
   - *preconceived ideas of what the other person is going to say.*
4. *Paying attention and being in the here and now.*
5. *Making it evident that you are paying attention, by verbal and physical signals.*
6. *Looking carefully at what you hear, understanding and analyzing it.*
7. *Getting anything clarified and explained that you do not understand.*
8. *Getting across 'message received and understood', when you have.*
9. *Expressing appreciation for the information given.*
10. *Asking for clarification, summarising what you have heard and being prepared to be corrected*

You tend to ignore what you don't value - if I feel or think that you are ignoring me, I get the message that you don't value me or my ideas.

The bad listener

This is an example from business life, where I am your boss and you are trying to communicate with me. What I am thinking is in italics. It could just as readily be a tutor and a student, or a parent and a child.

I am not paying attention. One reason is that I am worried about the Board Meeting to-morrow. I am not very much in the here and now. What's more I can't stand the way you keep on wagging your finger and emphasising every other word. My secretary comes into the room. 'Yes, come in and take these papers Susan'. 'Sorry about that interruption but do go on' *I know what you are*

75

going on about and disagree with it all. I am now working out what |I am going to say when you shut up. I am also wondering what that noise is, that is going on outside.

I am certainly not appearing receptive, relaxed, happy to be listening to you. I don't like you and I am making this fairly evident by the expression on my face and my body language, which I hope conveys to you that I am not going to be affected in any way by what you say. Even now I am glancing at a paper on my desk.

You certainly can talk. I'm beginning to feel angry at your impertinence and thoughtlessness. Perhaps I don't understand. Perhaps I don't want to. If I did, I might ask you to explain one or two things. Why I keep nodding, I don't know. You might think I am agreeing with you but it is actually my way of blotting out the unacceptable ideas you are proposing. 'Oh, there goes the 'phone again - I must answer it.'

I can't help yawning. The drinks and heavy lunch haven't helped. I think I will bring this to an end. 'I think I have indulged you enough. I've got some important things to attend to now, OK. Come and see me in a month's time and we can have another talk'.

What did I do wrong?

I was not in the here and now. I was concerned with your appearance, mannerisms, gestures etc. I was distracted by what was happening. I was concentrating my thought on my next reply. I was disagreeing - not openly, but internally - with what you were saying. I did not convey a Positive attitude to you, such as appearing receptive, relaxed, happy to be a listener, keen to hear what you had to say. I did convey that I was not prepared to be affected by what you were saying. I did not let you know that your messages had been received and understood. In fact I thought I knew what you were going to say so I didn't actually listen to you - but I did keep nodding as though I did. I certainly didn't ask any questions. I was tired and showing it.

It is not surprising that your relationship with me has taken a hard knock and that you feel unmotivated to serve my interests.

CHAPTER 7

MAKING FRIENDS - RELATIONSHIPS AND CONTROL

Making friends

Is a friend someone you like, get along well with, someone who likes you and doesn't disagree with you? Or is she or he someone who is always honest with you. Criticism, even from the friendliest of souls is not always welcome. George Canning said 'But of all plagues, Good Heaven, thy wrath can send, save me, oh save me, from the candid friend'. Is a true friend someone who doesn't criticise, who supports you, speaks up for you, stays loyal through both good and bad times?

When we talk of friends, we may have in mind many sorts - the people next door, some of the members of your school, college. club, people you meet on holiday, your relations, partner. Some of these are not necessarily what you would call friends but acquaintances. But you feel they are all friendly in so far as you feel comfortable with them. It does not necessarily mean that you have forged a strong relation with them. You just want to have people to do things with, to talk and pass the time with. The ideas in Chapter 6 should help you to do this.

However, if you have someone in your sights who you think is part of the plan you have developed in Chapter 3, you are probably going to get involved in a new relationship. In any event, you probably are already involved in relationships which you believe could be improved. What follows is intended to help you to understand the mechanics of relationships and for those relationships you are involved in, how they stand and how they may be improved.

So, what is a relationship?

If you say to me, 'I have a good relationship with you', which of the following do you mean?

- That you like me?

- That I like you?

- That I do as you wish?

- That I can make you do as I wish?

- That you and I communicate well together?

- That we never disagree about anything?

There is some element of relating in all these examples. If you like me, it is possible that this will affect me and to this extent there will be a flow of feeling from you to me. A connection will have been established and something will have flowed through it. The same reasoning applies if I like you. If I do as you wish, or you do as I wish, there is clearly a stronger interaction and a more powerful communication flow.

These possible meanings of what is and what is not a relationship are but a few amongst many possible valid interpretations. To attempt greater precision, I have turned to the field of physics and mathematics, where the word has a fairly precise meaning.

The mathematical concept

A simple illustration of what is involved in a relationship is the way a spring balance works. If you increase the weight on the spring, it gets longer. If you reduce the weight, the spring gets shorter. As long as you do not strain the spring, there is a very exact relationship between the weight you put on the spring and the amount it extends. If you double the weight, you double the extension: Halve the weight and you halve the extension. This is why it is possible to set up a scale in lbs. or kilograms - in lieu of inches or cms. - to measure weight in terms of the extension of the spring.

You can have an exact human relationship like this with someone, if her or his behavior is always completely predictable. For example, it is possible you can always rely on me to get angry if you mention a particular person's name - say, Hannah.. It is like a Sergeant-Major shouting 'left turn' to a well drilled squad. It is like switching a light on and off, when the switch is working properly.

However, often a relationship is not exact. There is uncertainty about what is going to happen at the receiving terminal. I may sometimes get angry when you mention Hannah's name, but sometimes I'm unaffected. The Sergeant-Major may have the same experience with a bunch of raw recruits. He shouts 'left turn', but some of them turn right. If the electric switch is faulty and you switch to the 'on' position, sometimes the light goes on and sometimes it doesn't. It is suggested that all these are called 'partial relationships'.

At the other end of the scale there is the nil relationship. You cannot make the other person do anything at all. Whatever you say has no effect. The Sergeant-Major says 'left turn', but the squad has mutinied and marches off into the distance oblivious of whatever he shouts. The electric light switch is completely broken, so that whether you turn it 'on' or 'off', it makes no difference.

These relationships or interactions may become less than exact or to some extent faulty, because you or the other person fails to communicate or to listen effectively. Or it may be that the conversation between us takes place in a noisy environment so that your remarks about Hannah are not always heard clearly by me. The squad may be drilling on a very windy day so that not all the members of the squad hear the instructions. The wire between switch and lamp may be faulty. However, probably the main reason why relationships are sometimes inexact is because one or both of the two people involved decide that it shall be so.

Relationship and control

Control is a familiar concept, but it is also an emotive one. Control of physical things does not usually involve psychological problems. For example, if you drive a car, and you are in control, you make it do what you want it to do. What about when you lose control - maybe the brakes fail as you are going down a hill, maybe the computer crashes? When this happens you cannot make the car or the computer do what you want. Such loss of control generally results in emotional reactions.

When we apply the concept of control to people, it can have a Negative feel. We talk of control freaks. We rebel against the idea of being controlled unless the idea appeals to us. So we use the term influence when often we really mean control. In fact we are controlled by someone or something most of the time. Certainly with ourselves there is a lot of control going on - our mind controls our body. **You** mostly control both of them. Your boss gets you to do things. Traffic lights control you. The weather controls you. Wanting to make money may control you. We are not as free as we might like to think we are

The word 'control' can be thought of as another way of saying 'relationship'. If you have control of your car, you have a relationship with it. If the brakes fail, you lose some, but not necessarily all control and the relationship you have with the car is only partial at best. So, where there is a relationship that is active, there is control. Where there is no relationship or the relationship is inactive, there is no control and there is a potential problem. Where there is a partial relationship, there is some control. There is also some absence of control and to the extent that this exists, there is a potential problem. This partial control situation is often what we experience when we talk about exerting an influence. Where there is a complete 100% relationship in the mathematical sense and the communication flow is active, there is complete control and there is no problem.

Thus the Sergeant-Major has 100% control over the well drilled squad, something like 80% control over the raw recruit squad and 0% control over the mutinying squad.

It is also important to see that control brings with it responsibility. If you have total control, you are totally responsible. If you have influence you have some responsibility. If you have control and you lose it, you may, or may not, be responsible for what happens as a consequence. Some people want to have their cake and eat it - they do not want responsibility but want to exercise some control. Control is power and power is what many individuals seek, often to avoid losing what they already have or to have more, so that they thereby feel safer. You may say 'I don't want to control my friends', but you may try to influence them from time to time and if you do so, you must accept responsibility if your influence is effective.

One-way and two-way relationships

Sometimes the flow between two persons communicating together is one-way. For example, if you are listening to a speech on the television, there is a flow from the speaker via the media to you but no flow from you to the speaker. But if you are engaged in a conversation on the telephone with somebody, the flow between you and the other person is two-way.

Similarly, a relationship can be one-way or two-way. Given that you and I have a relationship, there are three possibilities:

I can influence you but you cannot influence me

You can influence me but I cannot influence you.

These are one-way relationships.

Or I can influence you and you can influence me. This is a two-way relationship.

The extent to which I can influence you or you can influence me, can vary from complete control, through varying degrees of partial control down to almost nil control. It will also certainly depend on any formal ascendance that is built into the situation - such as boss-subordinate - or informal ascendance that exists such as buyer-purchaser.

And this extent may also vary with time or may depend on what the control or influence is about. In other words, I may be in a masterful mood one day. A few days later, I also may be very dominant when it comes to discussing sport but you may be the one with the business mind, in which area you call the tune.

The Sergeant-Major and the light switch connections are examples of one-way relationships. The Sergeant-Major makes the well drilled squad do things but the squad cannot make the Sergeant-Major do anything. The switch turns the light on and off but the light cannot do anything to the switch. However, if the relationship between Sergeant-Major and squad is partial, it becomes two-way - in other words, the squad of new recruits may have a substantial effect on the temper, and possibly the actions of the Sergeant-Major. But if the relationship between the switch and the light becomes partial,, it remains a one-way relationship i.e. there is nothing that the light can do that will affect the switch.

A two-way relationship can be illustrated as two people on opposite ends of a see-saw, making it see-saw.

For a human relationship to be effective, it appears necessary for it to be two-way. The strength of the relationships, however, need not necessarily be equal. For example, I may influence you a good deal more than you influence me. The propensity of one person to influence and control another appears to depend on a number of factors including morale, self-confidence and an extrovert drive to make things happen. As already mentioned, authority may be built into a position a person may hold or the role she/he may be playing. It may be achieved by force or earned by performance.

There is thus an equation, in terms of control, that satisfies the needs of the two people in the relationship. It seems to be a fact of experience that this equation has to be satisfied, not necessarily immediately, but in the long run. If it is not satisfied openly in the relationship, then it becomes satisfied in some other way which might appear to be accidental but which, nevertheless, redresses the balance of the relationship. For example, someone who feels unable to exert overt control may develop psychosomatic illness which has the effect of controlling the partner. Employees feeling an inability to exert any control on the management, may go on strike. A child may wet the bed or refuse to eat. Often the solutions to problems of this sort can be suggested by analysing the control relationships.

Being willing to be influenced and controlled

It follows from the above that an effective two-way relationship requires there to be a willingness on the part of both parties in the relationship to be controlled to a greater or lesser extent.

This idea is often embodied in the training of youth, and particularly in the armed forces where discipline is a basic ingredient, the inclusion of which is often justified by 'if you want to discipline, you have to be prepared to accept discipline'. It is evident in non-human relationships. You cannot sail a sailing boat without conceding some control to the wind and the tides. Whilst the boat is on it's mooring with the sails flapping and the waves slapping against the side of the boat, you have 100% control but nothing is happening. It is like the heavy man on the see-saw who will not allow it to move. To get something to happen, you have to cast off and allow the wind to fill the sails. The boat starts to move and, provided you have the skill, you can use the sails and the rudder to make the boat go where you wish. Even then control is not absolute. You cannot always go where you would like and may have to choose a destination consistent with the wind and tide, your capability and that of the boat.

Someone who refuses to be controlled or influenced at all is opting out of human relationships and may be a dictator, an authoritarian who gives orders and expects them to be obeyed but is not prepared to be told what to do in any circumstances. In some situations, for example, in conditions of great danger or distress, it may be essential for someone to take command and give orders. The perpetuation of this as a permanent style is likely to end in tears. The dictator can get away with it for quite a long time either by delivering a continuous supply of successes or by setting up a police state and a reign of terror, but history tells us that the inevitable end is disaster. Control implies the use of force and one important law governing forces was enunciated by Sir Isaac Newton - namely that 'action and reaction are equal and opposite'. And it is so often apparent that, as Lord Acton said, 'Power tends to corrupt and absolute power corrupts absolutely'.

Often relationships are seen as involving either 100% control or nil control, but with nothing in between. How often someone says 'Either I have complete authority to do what I want or I don't want anything to do with it at all'. An authoritarian management may conceive of itself as having 100% control with employees doing as they are told. This situation tends to encourage the development of a body of employees which sees the only solution as taking 100% control themselves. One way of doing this is to strike. Another is to refuse to co-operate. Revolutions against a tyranny often end up with another one.

The willingness of a person to be controlled depends on:

- Agreement with what she or he is required to do or believe.

- Belief in the competence and rationality of the person exercising control.

- Absence of or tolerance of any Negative feelings about being controlled.

Being willing to influence and control

Each person in a relationship has to exercise some influence if it is to be a real relationship and this inevitably implies accepting some responsibility for what happens, taking credit where it is due but also accepting the 'slings and arrows of outrageous fortune', the criticisms from others and oneself, taking it on the chin, accepting what happens and taking decisions - these are the costs of entering into a relationship. If one is unwilling to pay these costs, and to accept responsibility for causing the person, with whom one has a relationship, to do what one wants, and for the consequences that follow, then sooner or later the relationship will be damaged, probably irreparably.

There is often another cost in exercising control over someone. She/he may not necessarily want to be controlled and may react emotionally. It may seem, and actually be, that the relationship itself is in danger, A judgment has to be made as to whether the control one is exercising is beneficial to the other person and at a level that is acceptable in the long run. Clearly, it may only be acceptable in the short run with a lot of protest and pain - or it may not be acceptable at all. This is typically a parent/child situation. The parent may back off exercising the degree of control that is best for the child, for fear of losing the love and dependence of the child.

The need to take up a position of requiring 100% control or of nil control may sometimes indicate psychological problems. A common example is someone who talks incessantly and does not listen. This may be temporary. For example, someone may be angry and determined to get her or his own way, or afraid the boat will tip over and therefore feels it is urgent to take command. There are situations where it may be rational to take command. The boat may really be in great danger. Similarly, there are occasions when yielding up complete control is sensible, for example, if one is ill in hospital. It may also be pleasurable.

Being able either to exert or accept control should normally be rational and necessary experiences. Being unable to control can induce fear and panic and all sorts of psychological difficulties. Being unable to accept control implies a lack of trust or faith in the other person. It is a message in itself.

The control agreement

When two people are in agreement, the question of control does not arise. Control, in the form of influence may be involved in reaching agreement but once it is established, it is self-control rather than external control which ensures that agreed action is taken.

Where it is not possible to reach agreement about decisions, it is often possible to reach agreement about control. 'I will do it my way in this area and you can do what you wish in that area'.' If you do as I wish on this point, I will go along with you on that point'. Negotiations are a form of control agreement, as are contracts. Something I want, say money, is negotiated for something you want, say a house.

Communication as a control agreement

When good two way communication takes place, there is a control agreement. If you are talking and I am receiving and doing as I should, then I am listening attentively in real time, in the here and now and am content and happy to be doing so i.e. I am willing to be controlled to the extent that I take aboard what you say, look at it, understand it and let you know this has happened. You are in control. You have, temporarily, control of my mind with all the responsibility that this implies. You may tell me something that may be shattering or that may give great pleasure and be enriching.

If communication is all one way and you do all the talking, then the control agreement breaks down. Sooner or later I will switch off. In a good communication, there is an open or implied agreement to share control - not necessarily 50/50. It may be that 80/20 is acceptable. If it moves to 90/10 or 95/5 in your favour, I will only be talking 10% or 5% of the time and I will feel under pressure to get my messages across. I may be forced to make short, powerful statements which may come over to you as aggressive and which may stimulate such emotion in you that the control agreement is lost and a 100/0 situation arises.

Where there is no control agreement, communication is often impossible. If you and I are both intent on having 100% control, effective communication is ruled out. There are many situations where one person has 100% control and everyone else listens – for example in a lecture or in the armed forces. However, this should be followed by something like a 50/50 exchange of views, if agreement and self-motivation is to be achieved.

Self Counselling No. 7.1 Relationship assessment

The pattern of your relationships provides a broad description of where you stand in the world. It is useful, therefore to have a look at them from time to time and to decide, for example, whether they are improving and how you see them developing in the future. You probably have various circles of relationships - your family, friends, colleagues, and the people you need to make friends with and influence. How you move them from one position to another is what this book is about. But the first thing to do is to make an assessment.

Relationships are often complex. The strength of the relationship and the balance between one person and another will probably vary depending on the situation, subject, time etc.

If you and I are in a relationship, and I am making the assessment. To assess the strength of our relationship:

1. I assess how often you can get me to do what you want. Express this as a percentage (e.g. 40% of the time). Call this A
2. I assess how often I can get you to do what I want – as a percentage. Call this B

The strength of our relationship is $(A + B)/2$

The balance of the relationship, as far as you are concerned is $A/(A+B)$ and as far as I am concerned is $B/(A+B)$.

This assessment is how I see it. The above exercise can be repeated from your point of view. It can also be assessed by me as to what I think would be ideal

As an example, my assessment of the strength of our relationship is

1. How often can you get me to do as you want? Say my answer is 80%

2. How often can I get you to do as I want? Say my answer is 70%

Then my assessment of the strength of our relationship is $(80 + 70)/2 = 150/2 = 75\%$

The balance of the relationship as far as you are concerned is $80/(80+70) = 80/150 = 53.3\%$

The balance of the relationship as far as I am concerned is $70/(80+70) = 70/150 = 46.7\%$.

Ideally, you might wish the relationship to be stronger, say 90% rather than 75% and the balance more in your favour say 60%.

The above is my assessment. If you were to repeat what I have done, you may come up with different figures. If they were very different, this could highlight a disagreement that needs resolving.

For the persons you listed in Self Counselling No. 3, it will be useful to complete the following

Self Counselling No. 7.2 Improving a relationship

Think about and list the persons with whom you wish to improve the relationship

For each person:

* Do you want more control?

* Does she/he want more control?

* Can you expand the areas of agreement?

* Think about and list what they are and how you can do this.

Where you cannot expand areas of agreement, can you reach agreement about control

* territories?

* topics?

* other?

CHAPTER 8

YOUR AND OTHER PEOPLE'S IDENTITIES

Your and other people's identities

As part of your preparation to connect and interact with someone, it is helpful, to think about the identity and point of view you are going to adopt. Make sure that you will avoid being locked into a point of view or entangled in an identity which could frustrate what you are trying to achieve. Also think about the likely points of view and identities of the other person. How might you move her from her/his point of view? What you must avoid is for her/him to become entangled in an emotional identity e.g 'I am very angry', 'I have been insulted'. 'Once again I have been made a laughing stock'.

It is also possible to push people into identities - 'She made me feel stupid'. 'He made me feel like a child'. 'She made me feel like a king'. Doing so might be advantageous if you can push someone into an identity helpful to achieving your objectives. This is a technique often used by salesmen. For example, some salesmen will address you as 'Doctor' or will suggest some prestigious identity which you may be too flattered to disown.

It is possible to attribute incorrect identities to people. Often identities are guessed at from appearances or environments. You may see a man with a beard and a moustache wearing tweeds and a British warm and you may attribute an identity to him of a retired senior military man: whereas he is actually a retired bus driver. Guessing people's identities in a restaurant or on holiday is good fun, but if you have the courage to check whether you are right, you will frequently find that you are not.

In practical terms, attachments and identities are unavoidable. To be non-attached might be a religious objective for a contemplative but for those who are in what is called the real world, it is necessary to have agendas, angles, points of view and identities. What is essential is to be aware of your ability to be separate from these and to avoid being entangled or stuck in them.

Then you can examine them and see if they make sense. You can be the Naked Counsellor.

Identities may be permanent or transitory. For most people, identities are assumed and discarded all the time but some of them, such as the psychological types, formulated by Jung and described below, may endure.

Three important identities

From the multitude of possible identities, three are of special importance in that they occur with everyone. They are the identities of the CONTROLLER, the INFLUENCER and the COMPLIANT, any one of which we may assume at any time

The CONTROLLER is an identity of having or wanting nearly, if not totally, 100% control. Most people some of the time, behave as if they possess power and authority. They may have authority vested in them from the job they hold or position they occupy. Often they don't actually have it - they just need to feel in control. This can stem from feelings of inadequacy and Negative emotions. The CONTROLLER can be either Positive - loving, kind, gentle, nurturing : or Negative - oppressive, unkind, brutal, and destructive.

The COMPLIANT is an identity of being controlled and having very little or no control. The COMPLIANT can be either Positive - good, thoughtful, obedient, constructive, happy, or Negative - mischievous, troublemaker, irresponsible, disobedient, unhappy. Being controlled and having little control is often felt to be unpleasant and frequently gives rise to emotional behavior, which we may label as 'childish'.

The INFLUENCER is someone who is objective, rational, reasonable, logical and sensible, bent on reaching accord, making the assumption that others are Positive. She/he is prepared to try to influence and is willing to be influenced. She/he recognises that she/he will share control, not necessarily equally but certainly to have less than 100% control and more than 0% control

At any point in time, you can be one of a Controller, Influencer or Compliant. If you are being objective, you are probably an Influencer. If you have feelings of fear, or frustration, it may be that you are identifying with the role of Compliant. If you are identified with the Controller, then you are responding automatically as if you were the boss. Individuals can move from one identity to another quite rapidly.

Exchanges between Controller, Influencer and Compliant.

A communication exchange can be thought of as an ongoing communication between two people. such as a sale, negotiation or discussion. For effective, rational two-way communication to take place in an exchange of views, the amount of control exercised by the two participants cannot exceed 100%. This does not mean that if the attempt is made to exceed 100%, some communication will not take place but the outcome will probably not be what is intended. The examples that follow should make this clear

Either person in an exchange may be being one of CONTROLLER, INFLUENCER or COMPLIANT and treating the other person as if she/he were one of these three identities.

A typical exchange may involve me being a Controller and treating you as a Compliant. If you are willing to be a Compliant, treating me as a Controller, then communication and interaction are possible. I may be a boss ticking you off for some mistake you have made and you are prepared to be meek and contrite because you want to keep your job and you accept that you made an error. You respond respectfully and agree to take aboard my advice and not make the same mistake again. I have approaching 100% control and you have very little. The total amount of control we both have when added together is 100%, which satisfies the condition for effective, constructive communication.

An alternative exchange may be me being a Controller and treating you as a Compliant but you are also being a Controller, treating me as a Compliant. I am ticking you off but you are fighting back, saying that what occurred was my fault. I say 'You listen to what I am saying'. You say 'I am not interested in what you are saying. You listen to me'. Neither you nor I are listening. We are both getting angry. Useful communication cannot take place if the amount of control each person is attempting to exercise, when added together, exceeds 100%. The amount of control we are trying to exert between us in this situation is approaching 200% - which argues that no constructive communication can take place. Listening involves accepting some control and so, in this situation, neither you nor I are listening

Another greater than 100% control exchange would be if I were being a Controller treating you as a Compliant whilst you were being an Influencer treating me as an Influencer. I am not willing to listen to reason. I want

100% control and am in no mood to listen to logical, sensible talk. Effective communication is impossible because you are unable to exert any influence. This is an exchange in which it is evident that the amount of control both parties are trying to exert exceeds 100%, and it is vitally important when this happens, to be aware of it and to do something about it.

So if I am being a Controller treating you as a Compliant, the only way for you to maintain communication with me is for you to treat me as a Controller, and the only way to do this so that it carries conviction is for you to behave as a Compliant, listening, not answering back, being conciliatory and contrite. If my communication is received and acknowledged, it ought to be that I will gradually move out of the emotional state, which generally accompanies the Controller and become more rational. Hopefully, I will become an Influencer and be prepared to share control. It is just possible that I will swing completely to being a Compliant treating you as a Controller. This you will find very confusing and you will then have to be the nurturing Controller and with luck you may eventually get me to be a rational Influencer.

Controllers can often be identified as being incessant talkers, seeking 100% control in the communication. Often it is a feeling of insecurity that makes someone behave like this. If this is so, it is necessary to react in ways that make that person feel more secure. These ways are generally the opposite of what the Controller's actions and behavior stimulate you to behave. So you have to cease to trust your gut feelings but to think your way out of the problem.

There are individuals who oscillate between being a Controller, wanting 100% control and a Compliant, wanting no control and no responsibility. An example is someone who is a dictator at work but a lamb at home.

Understanding and being aware of these identities, can assist you in achieving and maintaining communication at the Influencer, objective, untangled level, which gives you the best opportunity to achieve the objectives of your communications.

Self Counselling No. **8.1** *Controller, Influencer or Compliant?*

Date.........................Other person......................................

For every exchange of views you have undertaken in order to reach
agreement with your point of view:

What identity did you assume –
initially...................................Controller, Influencer or Compliant?
during the exchange..................Controller, Influencer or Compliant?
finally.....................................Controller, Influencer or Compliant?
What was the outcome?

Anything to be learnt?

Date.........................Other person......................................

For every exchange of views you have undertaken in order to reach
agreement with your point of view:

What identity did you assume –
initially...................................Controller, Influencer or Compliant?
during the exchange..................Controller, Influencer or Compliant?
finally.....................................Controller, Influencer or Compliant?
What was the outcome?

Anything to be learnt?

Date.........................Other person...

For every exchange of views you have undertaken in order to reach agreement with your point of view:

What identity did you assume –
initially.................................Controller, Influencer or Compliant?
during the exchange...................Controller, Influencer or Compliant?
finally.................................Controller, Influencer or Compliant?
What was the outcome?

Anything to be learnt?

Date.........................Other person...

For every exchange of views you have undertaken in order to reach agreement with your point of view:

What identity did you assume –
initially.................................Controller, Influencer or Compliant?
during the exchange...................Controller, Influencer or Compliant?
finally.................................Controller, Influencer or Compliant?
What was the outcome?

Anything to be learnt?

Jung's psychological types

Introvert and extrovert

The eminent psychologist, C.G Jung, in 'Psychological Types', described eight different types of people. It is interesting and useful to recognise which type is the person you are currently communicating with and for your approach to have regard accordingly.

He identified two differing attitudes to life, two modes of reacting to circumstances, which he called 'introverted' and 'extroverted',

Introverts tend to be thinkers rather than involving themselves in much person-to-person interaction and activity in general. They find relationships difficult. In childhood, they may be cautious and somewhat solitary. As adults, they are often less materially successful than their talents deserve them to be. They may have unorthodox and original ideas and flout tradition and formality. They tend to be Influencers when they do communicate..

Extroverts are outgoing, interested in, relating to and being dependant - on people. They enjoy being in the world and are Positive.. They dislike being alone and think introspection morbid. They are good communicators and often wish to exert control. They frequently achieve materialistic success, especially in the media.

Most people are a mixture of the two, being introverted some of the time and extroverted at other times but many tend to be more of one type than the other. It is possible to argue that introverts and extroverts find it difficult to get on and to understand each other, but also to recognise partnerships where an introvert and an extrovert compensate for each other's deficiencies. Society demands an extrovert appearance so that many people, particularly introvert men, have to project themselves as extroverts.

Jung's Psychological types

Jung identifies four functions which people use to relate to the world: thinking, feeling, experiencing sensations, and intuition. What Jung calls a psychological type is a person who reacts habitually in one of these ways.

Jung's thinking person is interested in facts and logic. She/he dislikes the irrational, and tends to be a sort of desiccated calculating machine, lacking bonhomie and sensitivity to other's feelings. If she/he is introverted, she/he is interested in ideas rather than concrete reality and lives in her/his mind. She/he is the absent-minded professor, not easy to talk to or communicate with, other than in terms of her/his own interests. If extroverted, she/he is interested in facts, how things work and how they can be controlled and is task orientated. She/he may be typically an engineer or scientist.

For Jung, for the feeling type 'it is in order to attach a proper value to something'. He contrasts this with the thinker, who is more concerned with making a judgement and reaching a conclusion. In human relations, a feeling person is people orientated and concerned with relationships. When extroverted, she/he is a good communicator and is popular. Introverted, she/he is aware that she/he is a spiritual being and operates in a caring, non-material way.

Jung's sensation type experiences life through the five senses and is often pleasure loving. There is much communication with the body and often the body rules the individual. There is less communication with the mind. When extroverted, the sensation is the thing and there is a great capacity for enjoyment. Introverted, sensation types experience sensations and may communicate their sensations in abstract or surrealist ways. They often have deep feelings, with sympathy for those suffering or in need and tend to be spiritually aware.

Intuition is involved when decisions have to be made with inadequate data and where there is partial or little in the way of relationships or control. The extroverted intuitive type takes chances and abhors safety and certainty. He or she loses interest once a problem is solved. The introverted intuitive type tends to be mystical and artistic in a strange way.

Jung therefore classifies people into eight categories - introverted or extroverted in each category of: thinking, feeling, sensual, intuitive. If, for the people you have to communicate with, you can identify which type each one is, it will improve your understanding of them and assist you in communicating, and relating.

Self Counselling No. 8 Identifying Jungian types

For each of those you identified in Chapter 3 and those you are currently communicating with

1. *Is she/he introvert or extrovert?*

2. *What Jungian type is she/he?*

3. *What actions or change of approach do you need to take as a result?*

CHAPTER 9

MOTIVATING PEOPLE TO DO WHAT YOU WANT THEM TO DO

Previous chapters have dealt with clarifying your objectives and listing the people who can help you achieve them; how to generate a positive success-seeking mind set; the secrets of successful communication; the mind, body, spirit relationships and a number of important identities; making friends and relationships.. To make all this work for you, you have to get people to want to do what you want them to do. Furthermore, you have to motivate yourself to make it all happen so that all that follows needs to be applied to yourself and your internal communications as the Naked Counsellor.

People can be motivated to take actions to satisfy their needs. Important needs in some sort of sequence of importance are needs for physical safety, freedom, food, warmth, shelter, sleep, love, social contact, relationships, psychological stability, status, wealth, power, self-recognition and esteem. A need may be felt for some relationship with God and/or with spiritual values - music, poetry, art, nature etc. Somewhere in this list are cigarettes, alcohol and drugs and consumer goods. The consumer society uses advertising to persuade people into believing that they have an almost infinite list of needs - larger house, car, second house, second car, antiques, swimming pool, horse, boat, foreign holidays ad infinitum - and that if these are not satisfied, that they must feel deprived and disconsolate. **For you to motivate me, you have to discover what I really need and then work out ways you can take to satisfy my needs.**

There are two sorts of motivators - those that are external to the person and those that are within the person. Ultimately, all motivation is self-motivation because, in the end, whatever comes at you from outside has to be turned into a decision on your part either to do something or to ignore it. The only difference between the so-called external motivators and the internal ones is that if the ultimate self-motivation depends on an external motivator, it will cease to be effective when the external motivator is withdrawn. Nevertheless the external motivators are widely used.

External motivators

There are two external forces or pressures that can be used to motivate someone.

Rewards or expectation of rewards – greed.

Punishments or expectation of punishments – fear.

These operate continuously in life, in dictating prices in a free economy, on the stock exchange, in the shops - in fact, everywhere and at all levels. Their effect is mostly in a range of mildly beneficial to mildly harmful. However, if the external motivators are very powerful - for example, a gold rush or a reign of terror, or are perceived as such even when they are not, then they address the Negative part of the person and the individual may become entangled. Irrationality, destruction and other Negative actions may result.

Material rewards - can be various. Money immediately comes to mind. It enables so many material needs to be satisfied. It is the motivator that is widely used in industry, for example, as payment by results, bonuses, promotions, gain sharing The money on offer has to be sufficient and even then it doesn't always motivate.. The goods and services that money buys can also motivate - a new car, dress, holiday, a superb meal. Flowers convey caring. Sex is another widely used motivator.

Material punishments or deprivations - can be a withdrawal of rewards, or actions to cause expectations of loss. Fear can motivate people to fight, to be destructive, aggressive, competitive, or to run away, and panic, or to be frozen and unable to act. It is very powerful. Threats of a loss of a job or a customer or someone you love are strong motivators. Society is largely controlled by regulations and rules which threaten punishments of loss of money or freedom, if their contravention is discovered.

The problem with using coercive external motivators is that once they are removed, the motivation ceases. Applied to children, often punishments have little lasting effect. Applied to criminals, the evidence is that the same is generally true. Newton's Third Law - 'to every action there is an equal and opposite reaction' - applies not only to the use of force, but also to communication, so that the harder and more forceful the communication is, the less likely it is to succeed in achieving its objective in the long run.

There are many situations and organisations where there is voluntary agreement to coercion. Voluntary coercion also exists in varying degrees in most human relationships, societies, and cults. Being controlled when you don't want to be is very different from being controlled when you are content for this to happen.

Psychological rewards if you are motivating me include:

1. Being recognised as being of worth and importance. To provide this reward you have to think through my worth and importance. Do you know enough about me to do this? Do you need to do some research first? Most people have things of which they are proud. Having convinced yourself of my worth, you have to think how you are going to convey convincingly your appreciation without it sounding like flattery. Your attitude, body language can reinforce the impression. Ask for my opinion and advice. In a meeting refer favourably to something I have said.

2. Being given opportunities to achieve and excel. Doing this tends to come naturally to a parent, a teacher or a sensible manager. These are the opportunities we all seek. What do I want to achieve? Is there anything you can do to assist?.

3. Being given opportunities to learn and grow. This is another sort of door that you might be able to open for me. Can you find out what I want to learn?

4. Being part of a winning team.

5. Being acknowledged, earning acclamation, being accepted, being listened to, being asked to advise.

6. Being given control and responsibility.

7. Receiving love and caring. This is probably the greatest reward you can give anyone. To have love in your heart for everyone can justify a lifetime of effort and contemplation. In practical terms it shows as loving and caring acts, anticipating needs

Psychological punishments are the opposite of the rewards. If they are to motivate they must be seen as something to be avoided. They are Negative in character. Criticism is perhaps the most widely used psychological punishment. It rarely succeeds in motivating but can be very demotivating. Most of us deserve it from time to time, but we do not like it and it tends to make us resent the critic. Being ignored is a substantial punishment. It is a message, that rewards are not on the menu. It can have a very negative effect on the person being ignored especially if the reasons for treating her/him so, are not disclosed.

What demotivates?

Human relations situations can often be greatly improved by reducing or eliminating demotivators.
Criticism, particularly if it is felt to be unjust, is probably the most common source of demotivation. It may arise as a result of poor communication, so that the person being criticised has not been clear as to the rules, objectives, methods etc. that she/he thought applied.

Demotivation can spring from initial assumptions about a person, say you. If these are that you are likely to be dishonest, lazy and stupid, things will be organised such that there will be many checks and inspections, you will be externally motivated and the desired activities will be made as simple and repetitive as possible. The net result is usually low morale and productivity. The alternative assumptions are that you will be honest, hardworking and sensible and if you are not behaving so, then there must be something wrong with the way the activities are organised.. For example, you may be demotivated by not being given responsibility. Without responsibility, there are no opportunities to achieve and to win acknowledgment for successes.

Questionnaire 9.1 - What motivators?

Who do you want to motivate?

What do you want her/him to do?

POSITIVE MOTIVATION

What material rewards would she/he like?

What material rewards can you offer?

What psychological rewards would she/he like?

What psychological rewards can you offer?

NEGATIVE MOTIVATION

What material losses would she/he want to avoid?

Can you assist in avoiding these losses?

Or do you wish to suggest that you could make these losses happen?

What psychological deprivations would she/he want to avoid?

Can you assist in avoiding these losses?

Or do you wish to suggest that you could make these deprivations happen?

So now summarise the motivations you are going to use

Generating self-motivation in someone, such as me.

An alternative to external motivation is the generation of self-motivation. The way to achieve this is by effective communication to achieve agreement, so that the motivation is to do what has been agreed. It often depends on someone seeing the expectation of long term gain rather than instant gratification. It is not always successful but it often is and it has the great advantage that it proceeds under its own steam.

So, seeking and achieving agreement is a fundamental and primary means of making things happen the way you want them to happen, of reaching your goals. Selling involves getting the agreement of the customer to buy. Advocacy is persuading the jury or the judge or the committee to agree with the argument of the client for whom the advocate is acting. The politician seeks the agreement of the electorate with the party's manifesto. A contract is an agreement involving money or some other tangible benefit, probably achieved by negotiation. The many daily transactions of life involve getting people to agree and co-operate together. It is the basis of forming a team or developing an organisation - agreement on common goals, sharing responsibilities and benefits, on means and ends.

While the benefits stemming from a striving for agreement stand on their own, the elimination or reduction of disagreement and conflict is also vital. Considered on a person-to-person basis, then if you and I are in disagreement, it means that each of us have ideas and objectives that are partly or completely opposed. This can lead to ill-feelings and emotional behavior, which in turn can lead to entrenched attitudes and a lack of reasonableness. This malevolent spiral can continue with even more disagreement and emotion. Thus a row, dispute, conflict flares up.

The effects of disagreement between two people are often as follows.

- Neither takes any action about the things they disagree about - 'If we can't agree, let's leave it'
- One or other takes actions that are opposed to those of the other. 'I am going to do what I want anyway'. 'If you do, I will do my own thing and if it frustrates yours, too bad'.
- One or both behave destructively.- 'If we can't agree, I'm going to close the whole thing down'.
- They get emotional and unreasonable, which further reduces the chance of reaching agreement. - 'You're a stupid idiot not to see the advantages

of what I am proposing'. 'If you are going to resort to abuse, perhaps you should come outside,' - and then the communication might become physical.

This reasoning also reads across to you personally. If you cannot achieve agreement within yourself as to what you want to happen, you will either do nothing or do things that don't add up and which may conflict with each other. A substantial amount of energy can be locked up in discord within you. If agreement can be achieved, energy is released by increasing the amount and quality of decisions.

It is apparent that disagreement often has to be overcome to achieve your objectives in life. Agreement leads to action and the creation of wealth and added value in the widest possible sense. It is Positive, frees you from unpleasant and distracting feelings and enables you to be more effective. Agreement is agreeable, and pleasant. If you want to project yourself positively into the world and beyond yourself, to achieve more and more, then you have to achieve agreement with more and more people, to build teams, relationships and accumulate colleagues.

What is agreement?

If you and I agree completely about something, then this means that we both consider our ideas and beliefs about something to be identical. We have the same ideas and beliefs in common. If you disagree completely, then we both consider that we have no ideas in common about the particular subject. Partial disagreement implies some ideas in common and some not.

The act of agreeing

The act of agreeing - of achieving agreement - is the intention to find as much common ground as possible. It involves all the skills of communicating - asking questions to discover what the other person thinks and believes and exchanging ideas. The opposite activity is that of differentiating i.e. an intention to discover all the things and ideas which are not held in common. It is not sensible to argue about facts that can be verified, but people do.

There are many strong pressures on an individual to be different, to stand out from the crowd, to be independent, creative, a one-off. The media are always on the look-out for someone who is sensational and frequently she/he is an abrasive, aggressive, hard character. Much of society copies what it sees and hears. The copying of role models is a form of agreement and loss of personal identity, although the new identity may be uncooperative and disagreeable. Agreement and agreeing can be thought of as involving a loss of personal, unique identity because it means a sharing of identity with someone else. For those identifying with aggressive role models, disagreement is a way of asserting their individuality.

If you consider that some view, belief or idea is a part of you, then to agree with someone about this is to share part of yourself. You may feel that it involves a loss of 'face'. However, if you can realise that **you** and your ideas and beliefs are two separate things, agreement need not assail your identity or standing and so it becomes easier and less threatening.

The anatomy of agreement

What one is concerned with is getting agreement about how things really are. In a relationship between you and I, you will have some ideas, based on personal observation, remembrance of previous experiences and, also some incorrect assumptions, beliefs and observations. I will also have some ideas, quite possibly based on an entirely different set of observations, beliefs, remembrances and assumptions. If you and I are intent on reaching agreement, we will both exchange all the information and past experience on which our ideas are based and will note those which we hold in common. In this way agreement is built up.

In many situations then there is:

1. the real situation, the nature of which is not clear, e.g. the attitude of a potential customer to a possible new product
2. Your concept or model of the real situation, based partly on past experience of what you believe were previous similar situations, partly on having, say, spoken to a few potential customers, partly on 'reason'.
3. My concept or model of the real situation, again based partly on past experience of what I believe were previous similar situations, partly on possible customer reactions and partly on 'reason'.

By pooling your and my concepts or models, the combined model is more likely to resemble the real situation. Where you and I disagree, then further investigations can be made and other opinions sought.

Keep in mind that powerful emotions may be involved, particularly if there is strong disagreement. Try to occupy my viewpoint, to be where I am coming from. Try some role playing by acting out how I am feeling.

Changing one's mind

Perhaps the most difficult thing for a person to do is to 'change her/his mind', i.e. to accept a view about reality which hitherto she/he has not held. This is clearly essential if two people are to reach agreement - as opposed to agreement to disagree and tolerate each other's opposing ideas. To change your mind, clearly **you** have to be in control of your mind i.e. you have to be able to say 'This is me looking at an idea' rather than 'This is my idea and therefore part of me'.

To agree or not to agree

Agreement can be oriented towards either Positive or Negative ends. Further, what the majority believes is right may not always be so. For example, in the Middle Ages, there was massive agreement about the belief that the sun rotated round the earth and that the earth was the centre of the Universe. It is therefore only sensible to recognise that although the end goal is agreement, that to ensure that agreement is Positive and sensible, some disagreements have to be tabled and overcome on the way.

Because agreement is pleasant and disagreement is the opposite, there is a danger that agreement is reached too readily - that there is a pressure, or even a compulsion to agree. In consequence, it may be that decisions are reached which someone may be committed to, because she/he felt unable to voice misgivings, or put forward facts or experience which would have influenced the decisions.

Equally, there are some who are naturally dissenters, who rebel against conformity and who take way-out points of view. If such people disagree, without making the effort to understand what others are saying and to explain their ideas, why they conflict and so on, then the effect is Negative

Originality often depends on discovering exceptions to the rules. People engaged in research will often take this point of view. Engineering training is often directed towards discovering flaws in a design or mechanism. The process of design is largely one of considering all the ways in which something

- a machine or mechanism or structure - may fail and designing features to avoid such failures. Thus the role and education of some people can bias them in the direction of seeking disagreement, and this bias can extend into the conduct of human affairs.

This often explains why such people are sometimes not good at human relations and confirms them in the belief that probably determined their choice of career at the outset, that people are difficult to deal with and that it is easier to control and achieve success with things.

Often a person engages in conflict because she/he has a chip on her/his shoulders or a grudge against society for some reason or other. The most dangerous person is the one who is basically inclined towards disagreement but who projects the appearance of being reasonable and friendly.

Misunderstandings

The deaths of Romeo and Juliet in Shakespeare's famous play were the result of a simple misunderstanding, of jumping to the wrong conclusions on the basis of wrong information which had not been carefully checked out.

Disagreement which stems from misunderstanding is particularly futile, but it is very common. It is important therefore, when disagreements arise, to ensure that all concerned have communicated effectively so that they all have the facts clearly in mind; and that, if there is a disagreement, everyone is agreed as to what it is. Then it is clear that the disagreement is real and that some means has to be found to resolve it.

Resolving disagreements - negotiations

In some instances, it is possible to agree to disagree. You might not agree with some thing I want to do, but if it does not affect you very much, or at all, you can be relaxed and go along with it without exacting a quid pro quo. Alternatively, you can walk away and leave the whole thing unresolved. Whether this is acceptable or not depends on the cost of so doing, such as lost opportunity, inaction and all the negative results of disagreement.

Where it does affect you vitally and there is some sort of cost in abandoning your point of view, or giving in, or conceding what I want, you can enter into negotiations. This is an agreement about agreements. 'I will agree with you about A, B & C, if you will agree with me about D, E & F'. Similar, but not quite the same, is an agreement to take it in turns to make decisions that the other person does not agree with. This is more in the nature of the continuing give and take that takes place in a good relationship, partnership or marriage.

Agreement is a major objective of communication. An intention to agree, on the part of those involved, is fundamental to the success of communication. This may not exist at the beginning of an interaction, but the good and successful communicator will work hard to establish it. Thus a competent salesperson establishes a warm, friendly, agreeable atmosphere, talks of pleasant things, finds common cause about peripheral topics - the weather, football, cricket, the poor state of the roads, for example. A pattern of reaching agreement - a succession of small agreements - starts the process going and everyone, in some way or another, then becomes a Positive, agreement-seeking salesperson.

Being in agreement with life and with what happens, accepting what you cannot change and agreeing with as much as possible, is a recipe for a calm and peaceful life. From such a base, you can go forward to promote agreement - as a dynamic activity, making things happen, achieving results, reaching goals and targets, helping others. Further, you can release tension and energy around yourself by identifying disagreement and working to eliminate it.

Trust

All of the above presupposes that you and I are telling the truth as each of us sees it and are being honest with each other. The moment someone suspects that someone else cannot be trusted, even though this may not be true, then effective communication and agreement become very difficult. To destroy or disrupt someone's communication, it is only necessary to prove or infer successfully the untrustworthiness of the person in question.

Lies confuse and cause feelings of insecurity. How much is true and how much is false? Although most communication is conducted in good faith, nevertheless, a certain amount of distortion of the truth or downright lying, does take place. What is more exasperating is that the habitual liar cannot believe anything that anyone else says to her/him.

All you can do is to communicate honestly, tell it as it is, and believe what you are told, unless it is apparent that there are contradictions and that things do not add up. When this happens, you can ask questions to try to get at the truth. You are then into the techniques of the detective - approaching the person and the subject from a number of different angles.

How to generate agreement.

Lack of agreement results from the following

1. A negative intention to create disagreement.
2. Misunderstanding and confusion…
3. Lack of information.
4. Lack of communication.
5. The existence of people in whose interest it is for disagreement to flourish.
6. Lack of trust

The generation of agreement then can be seen to require the following.

1. A positive intention to create and reach agreement.
2. Active efforts to discover misunderstandings and eradicate them.
3. Provision of as much accurate information as possible.
4. Identification of those who benefit from a particular disagreement.
5. An intention by all concerned to tell the truth as they see it.
6. Above all, the maximum amount of positive and agreement orientated communication.

Self Counselling No.9.2 Analyse your disagreements

The list of questions below have been designed to enable you to review the disagreements you have with individuals. This is particularly important if any of these are people you have listed as being involved in the realisation of your objectives. Resolving disagreements frees energy and lets action proceed.

Are you in agreement with yourself?
Do you have conflicting thoughts and ideas?
If so, what are they and how are you going to resolve them?

For each person you disagree with:

What is the disagreement?

Is it important?

Is there another way to achieve your objective?

Is the disagreement due to the following.

1.   *A negative intention to create disagreement?*

        On your part?   *On her/his part?*

2. *Misunderstandings?*   *What are they?*

3. *Lack of communication?*   *What is the problem?*

4. *Lack of trust?*   *Can you define the problem?*

If you answer 'Yes' to any of the above, what are you going to do about it?

Do you understand exactly where the other person is coming from?

Have you tried to put yourself in the other person's shoes?

Have you got all the relevant facts and opinions?

Is there anyone with a vested interest in maintaining this disagreement in existence? Who is she/he?

If 'Yes', what can you do to eliminate the influence of this person?

Can you make the person you are in dispute with, aware of the third party?

Summary

In practice, if you want to motivate someone to do something, you will probably use a combination of external motivation and the generation of self-motivation. The psychological rewards are important and benevolent in their effect. If you have very little power, few cards in your hand, you will be forced to depend largely on generating self-motivation in the person you are attempting to motivate. For example, ultimately customers do not have to buy. They have to motivate themselves to do so and, if you are a salesperson, you have to supply the facts and reasons for them to become self-motivated

CHAPTER 10

TWO MIRACULOUS SOURCES OF POWER

1. Love (Charity)

'Though I speak with the tongues of men, and of angels and have not charity, I am become as sounding brass, or a tinkling cymbal.

And though I have the gift of prophecy, and understand all mysteries, and all knowledge; and though I have all faith, so that I could move mountains, and have not charity, I am nothing'

1 Corinthians Chapter 13, verses 1&2.

Up to now, Self Counselling has been largely concerned with the techniques of achieving success by communicating, getting people to do what we want and by relating to them. Success may, and often does, bring happiness and contentment. But, as has already been said, it is evident that not all successful people are happy or content. So, how can you be both successful and happy and contented. This is what this Chapter is about.

The two sentences at the head of this Chapter begin to provide the answer.. Because the word 'Charity' has become associated with almsgiving, it has become fashionable to replace it with 'love'. But 'love' popularly covers a wide range of activities - such as sex, concern for the underprivileged, patriotism, desire, addiction - many of which are to a greater or lesser extent materialistic and self-seeking rather than spiritual. Love can be defined as being a special concept.

Love, in the sense of charity, is altruistic and unselfish,
Not seeking reward or outcomes.
It does not make demands.
It is the highest expression of human potential.
It is not an emotion but is spiritual.
It involves a particular form of communicating and relating,
Which is ultimately more powerful than any other.
Difficult to define, it is not difficult to sense or experience.
It is a flow from one person to another
Which is not just body language,
Not just words,
But a communion of spirits.

Love is unselfish in contrast to self-love.
It does not answer the Negative with the Negative
But with the Positive.
It is a will to peace and humility within oneself
And to patience and kindness towards others.
It casts out fear and liberates.
It embodies the idea of doing to others
What you would like others to do to you
And that the other person's ambitions and needs
Are as important to you as are your own.
Love can involve sacrifice and a negation of self,
Yet it can be consistent
With a Positive self image.
It is a concern for what we love.
It does not exploit another
Or profit at her or his expense.
It has tremendous power,

**The me within us that was discussed in Chapter 5
is love.**
Yes, **You** are love.
Maybe **you** have never realised this exciting fact.
Maybe **you** have never been able to separate **you**
From your mind and body,
Which are concerned with success and failure.
It is all too easy for **you** to think
That **you** are your mind and body

Rather than separate from them..
You are Universal Love.
Just try to absorb this idea,
Contemplate it,
See it as something real.

This is how **you** can achieve miracles
By allowing the love that is **you**
To move your mind and body
To reflect exactly who **you** are.
You can love the love that exists in all nature
And in every person in the world
And it will love **you** back.
Every person has a deep felt need to be loved,
Not for what they do
But to be loved without any conditions,
Just for themselves.
No one can resist love.
If you really and sincerely love someone
She or he will buy what you are selling,
Whether it be a product
Or an idea
Or just you.
But it has to be real heartfelt love.

Love is giving not receiving.
Some believe that giving
Should be disciplined to the extent
Of giving some of your income to charity,
Casting bread on the waters.
'As ye sow, so shall ye reap'
It is possible to take a small step at a time,
To invest a small sum of money in giving.

Love is unconditional.
It is giving without expecting any reward.
It has been the experience of many people
That love has had to be earned.
This is conditional love,
And is not the sort of love that you should cultivate.
If I love you, I am accepting you completely.

This is what 'You're Positive' means.
I am loving the love that **you** are -
Not your foibles or habits,
Your ideas, your appearance,
Your possessions, your mind,
But just the spiritual **you.**
Anyone is loveable even though
She or he may be unlikeable or quite awful.
You may recognise that her or his spiritual self
Is entangled by the body
And/or the mind and/or the Negative,
Possibly that you have some responsibility to help.
It is said that you cannot give or receive love
Unless you love yourself.
You can give and receive love
To the extent that you have separated yourself
From your mind, body and Negative.
Love is active not passive.
Love does things, is creative.
Strives to magnify life and the beloved.

If you want to persuade someone to do something - a theme of this Book
- make sure it is to her or his benefit and let your genuine love which is the
spiritual **you** become apparent and felt. Give of yourself and be generous, for
it is in giving that we become the makers of miracles.

----

*'Greater love hath no man than this, that a man lay down his life for his
friends'*

'My religion is kindness' - Dalai Lama

Love is the supreme goal of human relationships-
The reason for living, as the song says.
It is the antithesis of materialism.
It is the saving grace of the world:
Just as materialism has the potential to destroy.

Love is what you experience when you look at a flower,
Or a baby
Or a beautiful landscape,
When you listen to Mozart or Chopin;
Whenever, in fact, you feel yourself in the presence of the Infinite
And feel overwhelmingly grateful,
Always to be aware that you are a spiritual being,
And have unconditional love and benevolence in your heart -
For yourself, others and all things.
Try not to criticise or be Negative
But accept what happens to you
As being part of the Creator's plan for you.

Christmas

The children were still awake,
Although midnight
Was an hour away.
The kindly deception of Father Christmas
Was almost thwarted.
But stumbling in the dark,
The rustling packages were placed
At the foot of each bed
By a tiptoeing anxious father,
While the mother distracted the attention,
Of those we daren't fail to deceive..

We woke, concerned lest the children
Woke before us.
Heard their cries of affirmation,
Slightly incredulous for a second,
Then knowledgeable, almost matter of fact,
They had always known it would be so.
We ran to share,
The shivering excitement,
The satisfied hopes,
The open hearted happiness,
The need to thank no one
But a white bearded old man,
In a red cloak
Who had come and gone unseen.

'Love thou thy life beneath the making sun
'Til Beauty, Truth and Love in thee are one'   *Robert Bridges*

How do I love thee? Let me count the ways,
I love thee to the depth and breadth and height
My soul can reach, when feeling out of sight
For the ends of Being and ideal Grace,
I love thee to the level of every day's
Most quiet need, by sun and candle light...'   *Elizabeth Barret*
                                                Browning

Love is not love
Which alters when it alteration finds,
Or bends with the remover to remove:
O, no! it is an ever-fixed mark'
That looks on tempests and is never shaken;
It is the star to every wandering bark,
Whose worth's unknown, although his height be taken.
Love's not Time's fool, though rosy lips and cheeks
Within his bending sickle's compass come;
Love alters not with his brief hours or weeks,
But bears it out even to the edge of doom.   *Shakespeare*

Self Counselling *No. 10 Love*

List the things you want, need, demand that are selfish, i.e. will only benefit you

  Anyone involved *What?*

List the unselfish things that you do or plan to do

  For whom? *What?*

How often, on a scale of 1-10, do you appreciate nature - the trees, flowers, birds, landscapes, water etc.

How often, on a scale of 1-10, do you appreciate art and beauty

How much of the time, as a percentage, do you separate yourself from your mind, body and the Negative

Who do you love unconditionally?

How do you express this love

How much do you give?

     To whom?   *What?*

10.2. The Universal Intelligence

Look at the world around you - for example, the way that each cell in a flower is programmed so that it knows where it has to be and what it has to do - from being a minute bit of dust in a seed, to being, say, part of a flower, then part of a new seed. Consider that all matter is made up of atoms, each with electrons and nuclei. Consider that you don't see matter like that You see trees and people Somehow electrical impulses get into your brain so that you 'see' something that you call a tree. What is remarkable is that when I look at the same tree, my brain also receives electrical impulses and it also 'sees' something that I call a tree. And this 'seeing' the same tree is the same for every human being on earth. Then all this and art and music and scientific research are all taking place on a speck of dust in a vast Universe. And then where do ideas, creative visions, concepts, original thoughts come from?

It is difficult to avoid the conclusion that something has written the almost infinite number of programmes of immense complexity to make all this happen. Something has created it all. It can't be explained as evolution or natural selection although this may have played some part. There has to be some sort of Universal Intelligence. Those of a religious frame of mind will call it God, Creator of Heaven and Earth. The idea of God as a person is useful because we are used to communicating with a person. Whoever or whatever created the Universe may be as unlike anything we imagine. After all, the world as we see it is quite different from what the physicists say actually exists. So you can talk to God and what is actually happening may be some sort of spiritual communication with a spiritual entity which you can call Universal Intelligence. The word 'God' is used in what follows but you can substitute whatever name you like.

To communicate with God, the spiritual **you** can use your mind and words and all the ideas in this book.. It is possible to ask for whatever you want. The Gospels in the New Testament report that Jesus said 'Ask and it shall be given you; seek and ye shall find; knock and it shall be opened to you: (St. Matthew Ch. 7 verse 7). He also said 'What things soever ye desire, when ye pray, believe that ye receive them and ye shall have them' (St. Mark Ch.11 verse 24). By praying, Jesus meant talking to God. Note the condition 'Believe that ye shall receive them'. This is absolutely vital. It requires faith to have the certainty that what you ask for, you will get. This is the faith and hope that is in the quotation at the head of this Chapter. This is the colossal power that you can tap into. It is so simple. All you have to do is to believe in

God, ask Him for what you want to happen and believe that it will happen. From the moment you do this, give it no more thought. You have handed over responsibility to God. He will have heard you and you believe it will happen. Make absolutely certain that no doubts enter your mind - just have complete faith. Do not tolerate any loss of faith by being impatient, looking for signs, worrying about outcomes.

One asks 'Why should He care about me and what I want to happen'. I don't know why. I only know that it is my personal experience that from time to time, I have had a Positive response when I have asked for something.. I can only hazard the guess that it is because **you** and **I**, and the spiritual part of everyone else, are capable of being in communication with Him because of the astounding possibility that **you** and **I**, and the spiritual part of everyone else, are to some extent God. If this seems fanciful, remember the phrase that 'the Kingdom of Heaven is within.', that we are made 'in the image of God'. St Paul said 'We are the children of God: And if children, then heirs; heirs of God.' This speculation leads to the thought that if I am God then if I can talk to myself. I can determine what is going to happen. This reads across to the idea of positive affirmations that were discussed in Chapter 4.

You may not believe that you can turn water into wine or move mountains but there evidence to believe that some people can heal the sick by faith. When considering whether miracles are possible, we should remember that each of us is a miracle and what we are doing here is miraculous. It is just possible that if we had sufficient faith, that miracles might start to manifest themselves in our lives. Meanwhile, you can ask for what you want to happen and have faith that it will do so.

Other qualities of God, other than love, are power and creativity. These attributes are to be found in individuals in varying degrees. They are clearly attributes that you may desire to have more of - to be more powerful and/ or more creative. To the extent that you are made in the likeness of God, you are already powerful and creative but perhaps you have had insufficient faith to discover your potential - what we call faith in yourself. People who become famous as politicians, business tycoons, stars of the media and so on appear to have had a powerful and unwavering faith in themselves and their destiny. The question is whether this success is available to you, if you can generate the same. How you answer this question may well determine what you achieve in life.

Happiness and contentment.

Happiness is a joyous experience and the more of it you can get, the better. Beyond happiness is contentment, the serene feeling of being in harmony with everything in the world. Is it possible to achieve this at the same time as trying to be rich and powerful? It is evident that a lot of rich and powerful people are not happy or content, because, on their own, material riches do not bring lasting happiness. An upward change of one's level of wealth, like winning the Lottery, probably brings happiness in the short run. But after dining in the best restaurants, flying first class, staying in the smartest hotels, wearing the most expensive clothes, one may well say 'So what!'. These things do not overcome loneliness, lack of love, lack of real friends. Nevertheless, there have been and still are rich and powerful people who are happy and contented and it is the hope that you will be one of them.

Your ideas and thoughts

The following blank page is provided for you to write down your thoughts and ideas which may come to you as you read the Chapters of this book, or may just come from 'outer space' – that is they may descend upon you, as they do, without you knowing where they come from.

Notes

About the Author

Alan Thompson has spent a good deal of his life helping individuals to communicate and relate more effectively to achieve their goals and ambitions. He has accumulated a practical knowledge of life which he has summarised in this book. He has also had a wide industrial and commercial experience as director of companies and leading a team of management consultants. He is married with five children and lives in Devon. He is the author of several previous titles, including a book published by Robert Hale Ltd., a few years ago on *Buying and Selling Pictures Successfully*, and has contributed a number of articles to national newspapers and magazines.

Printed in the United Kingdom
by Lightning Source UK Ltd.
119709UK00002B/26

9 781420 881097